JUNK to GOLD

From Salvage to the World's Largest Online Auto Auction

As told by
WILLIS JOHNSON

Written by
MARLA J. PUGH

WESTBOW PRESS
A DIVISION OF THOMAS NELSON & ZONDERVAN

WestBow Press books may be ordered through booksellers or by contacting:

WestBow Press
A Division of Thomas Nelson
1663 Liberty Drive
Bloomington, IN 47403
www.westbowpress.com
1 (866) 928-1240

Photographs property of Willis Johnson

ISBN: 978-1-4908-1657-9 (sc)
ISBN: 978-1-4908-1659-3 (hc)
ISBN: 978-1-4908-1658-6 (e)

Library of Congress Control Number: 2014900662

Printed in the United States of America.

WestBow Press rev. date: 01/27/2014

To Joyce

My faithful supporter in the
foundation we have built

CONTENTS

FOREWORD

When Willis first told me he was going to write a book, I thought, *Wow! That's great! People need to hear his story.* Why? Well, I've met a lot of amazing people in my life, but I've never met anyone like Willis Johnson. From his service in the Vietnam War to the building of a multibillion-dollar business out of one auto scrap yard, his story is one of achieving the American dream. It's a tale I would've thought was a fictional story written for the big screen if I hadn't seen it unfold with my own eyes.

This is a story of a man who believes in hard work and treating people right. Willis always says things like, "If you take care of the company, the company will take care of you," and "Watch your pennies and your dollars will take care of themselves," and "Don't forget a lot of people are counting on us." These values led to his desire to have no debt on his balance sheet, to go public on the NASDAQ Exchange, and to build a great company from the ground up.

I remember when he learned he could take his company public and have money for growth and that he would never have to pay it back. Willis said, "Where do I sign?" Of course he knew it was going to be a lot harder than just signing his name. He was going to have to convince people that a forty-six-year-old with no formal education and an Oklahoma accent could not only take his small company to Wall Street but that he could win there.

In my lifetime I have seen a lot of people underestimate Willis or tell him it wasn't possible. Telling Willis it can't be done only fuels him to try harder. It's his nature to work hard, to try new, innovative approaches, and to eventually win. I think a trait most entrepreneurs share is the ability to try harder when others say it can't be done. Those that quit when the going gets tough never see what they could have accomplished, and those that try harder are America's greatest entrepreneurs—like Willis Johnson.

You know that old saying, don't judge a book by its cover? I certainly did that when I met Willis nearly twenty-five years ago. I was introduced to him by his daughter—my future wife. Looking at the game mounts on his wall and his cowboy boots, I figured he was an avid sportsman who surely liked to throw down a few barley pops now and then. I also didn't understand how anyone could make a living selling wrecked cars. It was just foreign to me and didn't make sense. Willis was a successful businessman living in Northern California, and all the successful business leaders I had seen were in real estate or high tech—or anything, for that matter, besides junk. I couldn't have been more wrong in my assessment; Willis didn't drink, hunt, or follow sports. What he did do was business. That turned out to be the only thing I got right about Willis—because I thought he must be one heck of a businessman to figure out a way to make money with wrecked cars.

Meeting Willis changed my life forever and set in motion my informal but invaluable business education. I had the opportunity to shadow Willis when I was very young and very impressionable. And fortunately for me, Willis was very willing to share his wisdom and experience with me, whether at work or relaxing on a weekend. I took it all in and still rely on his words to this day. He was just full of life. He didn't come home at seven at night with his shoulders down like he had just put in another day at the salt mine. His work didn't drain him; it drove him. I wanted to be like that.

Even great entrepreneurs make mistakes, but they only make them once because they learn from them. Willis was never afraid to take a risk, but when it didn't work, it was time to course correct. Making sure you learn from past mistakes was one of the best lessons I learned from Willis over the years.

This book is a collection of stories about trying new things, believing in your mission, and having a vision of where your industry is going and where you can take it. Willis used to say if you get big enough, you can make an industry behave in a particular way. Apple probably feels that way right now with the innovation of their iPhone, and while great innovators hate to be copied (Samsung), it is still the highest form of flattery and says to everyone you are doing it right.

With relentless commitment and hard work, Willis knew anything could be achieved and sometimes you may even exceed your own expectations. From his marriage to Joyce to the building of the greatest online auction company in the world, his is a story of exceeding expectations.

As you turn the pages, you'll realize that what you see in Willis Johnson is what you get; nothing more, nothing less. He purposefully wrote this book so that you would be able to see his character, his passion, and his soul. While this may be cliché by today's standards, he is a man of uncommon common sense. His love for family and friends is only exceeded by his love of, and faith in, God.

I know you will enjoy the chapters that follow, but more importantly, I hope you're inspired to take your own risks and discover that you are capable of doing more than even you may think possible. Willis loves to hear of people making their own entrepreneurial dreams come true, and I know he wrote this book in the hope you would believe that with God on your side, there is nothing you can't do.

—Jay Adair, summer of 2013

PREFACE

Make Your Own Way

Folks come up to me after speaking engagements and ask where they can hear more about my life and business philosophies. They want to know how I turned one auto scrapyard into a multibillion-dollar, global auto auction company. They are looking for a magic formula, maybe. I wish I had one to give. I don't think there's a formula, and it's not magic at all.

When folks tell you they've been in business their whole lives, they usually mean they've worked a long time. When I say it, I mean my *whole* life. It's something I learned from my dad, who taught me everyone should make his or her own way in the world.

My dad was the smartest man I ever knew in business, and I soaked up everything I could from him. We not only shared the same name but also a belief that nothing was impossible with hard work and determination.

And hard work it was. When I was growing up, my dad would often work fifteen hours a day, seven days a week. It was always that way for my dad. When he was a kid, he would fill a small wagon with ice and bottles of Coke. He'd take that wagon to construction sites and sell cold drinks to the workers. He learned the value of hard work, and it gave him a taste for starting up businesses that could help support the family.

Because my dad never worked for anyone else, the thought never crossed my mind that I should either. Besides, you never complain about your boss when you are the boss.

When I look back, I think my success is partly due to the lessons my father taught me and partly due to God's hand guiding me along the way. I also think a good portion of it has to do with the fact it never occurred to me that what I was doing might not work. I never thought I couldn't do it. Some may call it confidence. Some may even think that kind of blind optimism comes from ignorance. But I just never let the possibility of failure enter my mind. And I think when you can leap into something wholeheartedly like that, you can do amazing things because you don't have fear holding you back.

Maybe it was easier for me to do that because of my faith. When you have God on your side, it is easier to let fear go. I always trusted Him with my life and my business—and He never let me down. That's a pretty powerful business partner to have on your side.

This book is a collection of some of the lessons I've learned over the years—from my dad, from God, and from a lot of other really smart people along the way. Some lessons I also just had to learn myself. It's a little bit personal history, a little bit history of my company, and a lot of storytelling. I wish I could say it is the magic formula for success and if you follow it, you too can turn junk into gold. But every person has to find his or her own path to success, just like my dad said.

At the very least, I thought it was time to write some of this down—for my family, for all the employees who have helped me succeed over the years, and for the other businesspeople I meet with their own ideas of how they are going to change the world. I hope some of the lessons may be useful to you and that you may be inspired to have the faith to jump wholeheartedly into your dreams.

—Willis Johnson Jr.
Franklin, Tennessee

CHAPTER 1

Lessons My Dad Taught Me

> Take care of your pennies and your dollars will take care of themselves.
>
> —Willis Johnson Sr.

Earn a PhD in Common Sense

The time I spent as a kid with my dad was much more of an education for me than what went on between school bells.

When I was about twelve, I'd help out after school at the construction site my dad ran. As I swept and cleaned up, I paid attention to how my dad ran a crew, measured, cut, and hammered. He always seemed to get it right. I thought there was nothing my dad couldn't do.

Every night, Dad would sit down at the kitchen table and hand that day's newspaper to my mom. She opened up the paper to the classified ads and read the "For Sale" section out loud. Dad sat at the kitchen table, concentrating mostly on the "For Sale" or "Miscellaneous" sections. When Mom got to something that interested him, he'd say, "Now *there's* how I can make some money" and ask her to read it to him again. Then Dad would make some phone calls and put a deal together.

As my parents performed this nightly ritual, we kids were often in the living room, watching television and churning butter. We took turns shaking a gallon jug of cream until the liquid was almost gone and butter remained. In our own little way, we were churning out gold—turning cream into butter. Meanwhile, Dad and Mom were finding a way they could turn a classified ad into a golden opportunity.

It always fascinated me how my dad never missed a chance to make money. He was always focused on the next deal. It never even occurred to him that the next deal might not come or he wouldn't be able to make money at it—even if it meant he had to learn something new. I guess that's where I got it from.

It never occurred to Dad that he should learn how to read, either. There was no time for that, because he had a family to support. It was that way for him growing up poor in Oklahoma with twelve brothers and sisters. From a very young age, he was expected to help support his family. He had to drop out of school after the fifth grade to help put food on the table. Education was a luxury they just couldn't afford.

If Dad had been able to read, I don't know where he would have gone because he had a lot of common sense, which I really admire. For that matter, I didn't graduate from some Ivy League college either, but I did all right. Sometimes what they teach you in school just isn't as important as what you learn in real life, I think.

But as Dad got older, not being able to read did keep him from getting a decent job. He knew if no one hired him, he was going to have to continue to find ways to work for himself.

During the World War II rubber supply crisis, he drove from farm to farm, buying old tires for a nickel each and bringing them to rubber companies, where they would be recycled for a profit. He became very good at finding business ventures that could fill a need.

But as hard as he worked, Dad wasn't just about business. Everything he did was for family.

My mom told me that on the night I was born in Clinton, Oklahoma, she and Dad had been dancing a jig in the living room as my older brother and three older sisters ran around the house. The day I came home from the hospital, Dad had the ambulance play lullabies the whole way.

While it was a good life, it wasn't an easy life. Not knowing how to read just made things more complicated for my dad. When one of his businesses got so big that he could no longer keep track of the numbers in his head, he'd have to auction the business off and start something new. It meant we had to move a lot as he went from pouring cement to clearing snow, laying bricks, or installing underground pipes. Change became normal for us, a way of life. Before I was five, we'd go from Oklahoma to Southern California to Yakima, Washington. We had to learn to adapt. I think it made us stronger.

Embrace Adventure and Learn from Second Chances

When I was five, the family moved to Northern California near Sacramento, where we stayed the longest. I think this is also where my sense of adventure developed, which I would carry with me through business too.

For me, it was like being inside *Tom Sawyer.* I'd walk the creek beds in Rio Linda and the North Highlands with my buddies David Flower and Danny Boyd, taking off early in the morning with handmade bows and arrows, slingshots, and peanut butter and jelly sandwiches our moms had made. We'd walk for miles or drift on the creek in makeshift rafts, shooting frogs and fish and digging for crawdads as we told stories. Some of them were even true. We'd plan out our next great adventure as we cooked what we caught that day and had a feast on the creek bank.

David's father had built a concrete bomb shelter back then—a sign of the times when the United States and the Soviet Union were in the middle of the Cold War. It was a perfect place us to go and hang out all night. Not only was there food stockpiled, but it was also dark so you could never tell what time it was. We'd stay up all night in the bomb shelter, play board games, and tell jokes. Some of them were even funny.

David and Danny were very different but like me in some way. Danny was a radical and would try anything, even if it meant he might get into trouble. I like to try new things too, but I wasn't much for getting into trouble. That's where I was more like David. David was more of a follower. He would always do what you wanted to do and didn't like to ruffle feathers. So I was kind of in the middle. I'd keep

Danny from throwing rocks at street lights, but I was also willing to try anything as long as it didn't hurt anyone.

One time, though, we got in over our heads. Literally. We were about eleven, I guess, and floating on inner tubes in Lake Folsom. I lost my tube far out in the lake and couldn't swim. David came over to save me from drowning, but because I was panicking, and because he wasn't used to having to carry his weight and mine, he started to go under too. Then Danny came over to help, but his tube got away from him as well, leaving all of us just able to keep our heads above water in very deep water and a long way from shore. We knew we were in big trouble. Luckily, a boat full of eighteen- to twenty-year-old girls happened by and rescued us all. We thought they were our heroes, but they looked at us like we were kids and called us cute. Still, there were worse things than being rescued by a boatload of pretty girls.

I learned how to swim, though, after that. I figure if you're given a second chance, you should learn from it.

Don't Feel Sorry for Yourself

When the building industry fell apart in California in the early 1960s, my dad needed a new way to make money. It was time for another change, so we all packed up and moved to Arkansas, where my dad was born. We stayed at a cheap motel while Dad put his latest deal together—the purchase of a 150-acre cattle ranch.

It was hard to move to Arkansas. For one, I had to say good-bye to Danny and David. But I also had a hard time fitting in. I was about fifteen, and I liked to wear black, pointed-toe shoes and combed my hair into a pompadour. It was very James Dean–like. And it was the way most guys my age in California wanted to dress.

Arkansas was a different world altogether. I stuck out like a sore thumb. And in Arkansas, they also had segregated drinking faucets for blacks and whites. I didn't understand that. In California, no one cared who drank at what faucet. Weren't we all the same?

My sisters had a hard time too. The kids would make fun of them because they teased their hair like the movie stars did. Luckily, we had each other. We had moved so many times we learned the one thing you could trust would never change was family.

There was also no time to feel sorry for ourselves. We all kind of lost ourselves in hard work—which there was plenty of on the farm. My older sister, Regale, and I were told to put up fences around the entire ranch. It was a very big ranch. My dad showed us how to get started. Regale and I hauled planks, dug holes, and hammered nails for months. When that was finished, we then had to start all over again, covering every inch of the fencing we built with whitewash. There wasn't much I didn't know about putting up a fence by the time we were done with that.

Know What You're Paying For

Although I got really tired of building fences, I never got tired of going to auctions with my dad.

You might be saying to yourself that going to an auction wasn't exactly living the high life. But going to that old sale barn meant I would miss a few hours of hard work. Besides, the hot dogs were delicious.

I'd chew on a hot dog and look over the livestock while Dad would bid on the equipment he needed. Every now and then, though, there'd be something special. From time to time, Dad would bid on mystery boxes.

You see, the auction barn would have these storage bins you could bid on, but you didn't know what was in them. You'd put in your bid, and someone would take that box home with no notion of what was inside. Sometimes it was scrap. Sometimes it was gold. I tell you, if you get home with a box full of left shoes, you remember it. That's right—a whole box with single left shoes. That might not have been the best deal Dad ever made.

Another time we went to Yuba City to bid on items from a Grant's department store that was going out of business. Dad had hardly purchased anything—just a few racks and other things he thought he'd be able to resell for more money. He also bought a pallet of small boxes and told me to load them in a truck. I took a look at the labeling on the boxes and scratched my head. But like I said, my dad was a smart businessman; I figured he knew what he was doing. So I loaded up everything on the truck, and we headed home.

We pulled up to the house and climbed out of the truck. Dad was smiling from ear to ear. He proudly told Mom, "I bought something we can give the girls this Christmas. They're gonna love it. Makeup compacts!"

Well, Mom was excited.

I was confused. I'd loaded that truck after the sale. I hadn't seen any compacts.

I told him I didn't remember putting those on the truck. Maybe we missed something.

"No, no. See, right there. That whole pallet of little boxes. Compacts." He was proud to point out, "Now the girls can put makeup on anytime they want."

I looked back at the pallet. Turns out that if you can't read very well, every box is a mystery box, and C-O-M-P-A-C-T can be spelled T-A-M-P-A-X.

We laughed about that one for years.

Luckily, Dad hadn't spent a lot of money on the pallet, and of course, my sisters did still find a use for them. But it taught me a valuable lesson. Know what you're spending your money on.

Be as Relentless as the Cows

Tampax and left shoes aside, most the deals my dad made were good ones. One day he bought thirty Holstein cows and milking machines at the auction.

At fifteen, I didn't fully understand the implications. Holsteins had to be milked every twelve hours and would produce between four and eight gallons at every milking. If you didn't milk them, the liquid would run out of the udder, and they would begin to produce less. That meant that although the cows had been milked at five that morning, before we could take the cows home to the ranch fifty miles away, they had to be milked again by five that night.

It also meant that once we got the cows back to the ranch, we had to stay up all night, setting up the milking machines so the cows could be milked again at five the next morning. I still wasn't sure what Dad had gotten us into until I got home from school that afternoon and was told to milk the cows again. The cows were relentless. I knew then there would never be time for anything else, like sports or after-school activities. This was what I had to do.

When I turned sixteen, Dad bought me a new Chevy pickup truck, and my dairy duties expanded. To pay for the truck, I had to haul milk to and from the creamery. I would get up at 3:30 a.m. and milk the cows with Regale and then load the full milk cans in the back of my pickup. I ate breakfast and got myself ready before driving the milk cans to the creamery by 6:30 a.m. on my way to school. On the way home, I stopped at the creamery again, picked up the empty milk cans, and went back to the dairy to milk the cows again before bed. On the weekends, I'd tend to not only the dairy cows but also the beef cows. I might bale hay too.

Everyone Is Created Equal, but They Aren't Always Treated Equally

While hard work became second nature, I learned it wasn't always a guarantee of success, and people aren't always treated equally for equal work. The world was unfair, and this bothered me.

During my dairy hauls, I found out the dairy down the road was getting paid more for their milk. The other dairy wasn't cleaner or better than the Johnson dairy, and neither did they have different cows. In fact, the dairies often bought and sold cows and equipment to each other and were inspected by the same people. The milk from the two dairies was even mixed together at the creamery in one vat. The only difference between the dairies was that the other dairy had the permits necessary to classify it as a grade A farm, while the Johnson family dairy was a grade B farm. Because only a certain number of dairies can be a grade A farm, and there were no more permits available, no amount of hard work would change this.

I remember asking Dad if we could pay a neighboring farmer to use his vacant land to plant hay for our cows. That field was covered with weeds, and I thought it would be an opportunity to put land to good use. Dad explained that the farmer was paid a subsidy by the government to let his land sit idle. I didn't understand how that could happen. Wasn't America about free enterprise? Why did that farmer get paid for doing nothing while we were working hard to make ends meet?

While my dad taught me how to crunch numbers, build a business, and take chances, Mom played an important role in making me a leader. The most important lesson I learned from her was that no one was better than anyone else. The move to Arkansas, where people judged me by my hair and clothes, had taught me early on what it was like to be treated unfairly. The feeling of unfairness was reinforced when I found out about the disparity in prices between our dairy and the grade A dairy down the road. Mom's assurances that the Johnson family was just as good—but no better—than everyone else was one of my building blocks. I was able to approach life and people with confidence and treat others with respect. She set the example for me to have the strength to handle change and all the challenges that would cross my path.

Forgive and Forget

People say I'm a lot like my dad. Most of the time they mean that in terms of business. But we also shared a love of family and fun.

Whenever there was a break from work on the farm (and there were few), my brothers and sisters and I found happiness outside riding bikes and horses, shooting guns, and hunting and fishing. David Flower would sometimes visit me from California, and we'd always talk about girls. David also loved the farm and liked to help me play pranks on my younger brother, Curtis. One day we convinced Curtis that if he sucked hard enough on a cow's udder and then ran outside, he could see the wind blow colors. Curtis tried this several times before he caught on. David and I couldn't stop laughing at him.

Like my dad, I also liked to make my mom happy and buy her things. I'd ask if I could use trading stamps to buy her a cake plate, or I'd use some of the extra money I saved from working to buy her a ceramic knickknack I thought she'd like.

My mom tells me I'm competitive like my dad. I always loved to play card and board games like Monopoly or Risk because I could get a lot of money or conquer the world. Mom said I only liked to play the games I could win. That's probably because I never wanted to play dominoes with her. In truth, she would always beat me. Where's the fun in that? It was always much more fun to beat her.

People say I look like my father too. And although I did graduate from high school, I was never very good at reading or writing. But I was good at math, just like my dad, who had a natural head for numbers. He could figure out how long the third side of a triangle was based on the other two but didn't know what a hypotenuse meant. He could figure out what a number should be in a formula but didn't know he was doing algebra. He just instinctively knew how to apply numbers to practical situations, especially business.

I inherited some of my father's temper too, along with his sense of fairness. But I think because he grew up harder than I did, he was harder. If he said to shut the door and we hesitated, we'd get a spanking. He was too busy trying to support his family to have the patience for children who didn't listen. Luckily we knew this and didn't hesitate very often. His word was gospel.

Dad never shied away from letting people know if something bothered him, even if it meant hurting someone's feelings. If he thought you did something wrong, he'd get mad and yell at you, and you'd feel stupid for it. But he never held a grudge, and when he was done sharing his temper, you'd often never hear of it again. As a result, we were all raised to forgive and forget. While I have some of my father's temper, I am better at letting it out less publicly—usually behind closed doors. But like my dad, once I let it out, it's done. I'll never bring it up again.

Take Care of the Business, and the Business Will Take Care of You

Both my dad and I also built reputations in the business world of always standing by our word and never doing business if a deal felt wrong. We both walked away from opportunities that may have helped our businesses but would have crossed a moral or ethical line. To us, the business world was black and white, and a deal you aren't sure about isn't really a deal at all. It never ceases to surprise me, though, when others cross that line without even a blink of an eye. I was raised to believe that cheating is the same whether you are taking ten cents or $10,000. And if you could do it once, there was a good chance you would do it again.

My sister Bonnie said those ethics were what made me a leader. She said even when I was young, I'd speak my mind when I thought something wasn't fair and stand up for what I felt was right—just like Dad. Dad didn't like it when someone tried to cheat him, or someone else, for that matter.

Dad also had an expression: "Take care of your pennies and the dollars will take care of themselves." It's a phrase I have also passed on to others so they would learn the same lesson I learned from him—that small amounts of money can add up to either big profits or big losses. You can't ignore the small expenses or the small amounts of money unaccounted for if you hope to succeed at the end of the day.

Another phrase Dad used to say all the time was, "If you take care of your business, the business will take care of you."

One day my dad and I were in town picking up something. We walked past a brand-new shoe store that had just opened up. A man pulled up out front in a brand-new Cadillac. It was a fine car. The driver got out of the car, walked up to the shoe store, pulled out a key, and opened up shop. I guessed he must be the owner.

Dad looked down at me, and then he looked back up at that store.

"You think the owner of that store makes enough money to buy a Cadillac?" he asked me.

Well, seemed to me that a man buys the car that's right for him. I mean, we sure didn't have anything that fancy out at our place, but I imagined the storeowner must have been doing pretty well.

Dad looked at me and said, "He should be driving a car worth a third of that. And he should be putting all that money into the store."

Dad wouldn't say business comes before family. But it came before just about everything else. And he would tell you that if you treat the business right, it would have a better chance to support your family and put food on the table. It's tough to start a new venture, but once it starts to grow, you want to nurture it.

It's a little like raising a kid, when you think about it. When a baby is born, that little guy can't do much for himself. He's depending on you to take care of him. But you tend to him, feed him, keep him safe. And in a few years, he's standing up on his own and making his way in the world. Down the road, that little guy is grown and taking care of you.

A business has a little bit of that family feeling to it. You spend a lot of time with it, so you ought to treat it right. And if you treat it right, then it'll grow, thrive, and eventually take care of you. If you neglect it, though? Well, if you neglect it, it'll fail.

That shoe store? It stayed open for a little while, but then one day it was just shut down. Gone. I don't imagine the owner ever knew it, but my dad took one look at that Cadillac and could have told him what to expect.

A new piece of equipment for the farm always took precedence over new furniture or other extras. If I got a buck knife for Christmas, I was happy. I didn't expect anything more. And that was okay because we always had food on the table and a roof over our heads. Even as I became really successful and grew wealthy, it was never at the expense of my company. The company came first, and in turn, as it succeeded, it took care of everything else.

Don't Forget Where You Came From

One of my favorite phrases is, "Sittin' in high cotton." It means everything is going well. The cotton's high, which means the profits are too.

But I've found you appreciate sittin' in high cotton a lot more when you've had times you couldn't even find the cotton. It's those times that keep you humble.

Times on that cattle ranch in Arkansas were hard. Even though Dad kept us fed and clothed and scraping by, it was just that—scraping. Sometimes by the skin of our teeth.

My sisters would share one room in the farmhouse, while Curtis and I would sleep on the screened-in porch. We'd adjust by adding blankets in the winter and taking our shirts off in the summer.

We kids would only get new clothes once a year—before school started. The girls would get two dresses and a pair of shoes; the boys would get two pairs of pants, two shirts, and a pair of shoes. It would have to do.

We'd also get one set of church clothes, which Mom would dress us in every Sunday. Sometimes the entire family went together. Other times, when there was too much work for my parents to get away, my brothers and sisters and I would walk to church by ourselves in our brown suits and fluffy dresses. Mom insisted on it.

Mom was also raised on a farm with a large family and learned the value of hard work by picking cotton. But her childhood had been easier than Dad's, as her family had been better off economically. She was not only able to attend and complete school but was also encouraged to be active in the church.

Dad, on the other hand, had a reputation for being an ornery, hard-talking construction guy. Growing up, he never went to church, but to please Mom, he began to go. Eventually his sense of fairness and right and wrong was touched by the sermons he heard, and he, too, believed in God.

We needed our faith in God and in each other to survive. The weather had been bad in Arkansas the year I was sixteen, and there wasn't enough hay for cattle. My dad, never one to give up, put more deals together in an effort to supplement the family income. He even bought a bulldozer so he could dig out irrigation ponds for other farmers.

While that helped for a while, it was clear we would have to make another drastic change to keep putting food on the table. Dad decided to go back to California and held a big auction to sell the farm and all its assets. He even sold our collie dog and cats—which made my sisters cry. Looking back, though, it had to be done. Dad didn't know yet what California had in store for us, and a farm dog needed to stay with the farm.

While Dad was an expert in starting businesses, he wasn't as good at getting rid of them. He didn't realize he could sell his businesses for a lot more money and wasn't educated enough to figure out their true value. When he was done, he would just auction off the assets. But getting a business over the hurdle of making money is the hardest part, and being able to sell a business with a profitable track record and brand was worth more than just the assets alone. While a lot of businesses never see a profit, like that shoe store, Dad's businesses always did. But he never factored that into the sales price or tried to sell the business privately as a whole instead of auctioning it off in parts and starting another business from the proceeds.

Mom always supported Dad, his businesses, and the change that went with it. When Dad announced we would have to sell our house and furniture because he needed money for his next business, she wouldn't complain. She never knew what it was like to stay in one home for years at a time, yet it didn't seem to bother her. She trusted him to do what was best for the family. And he trusted her.

I would overhear Dad talking to Mom a lot about business and his plans. She was his sounding board and would listen when he needed her to. She'd also share her gut feelings about what was wrong and what was right—serving as his expanded conscience. I remember thinking even then that I wanted to find someone like that when I got married someday—someone who would support me and help me do what was right. And luckily, I did.

Everything Has Value

Back in California, we moved into a small subdivision in Elverta, where Dad began to bring newspapers home again in search of his next opportunity.

It wasn't long until an auction in Fallon, Nevada, piqued his interest. He told me and my buddy Rocky to jump in the truck and come with him to Nevada, where there was money to be made.

A construction company there had gone bankrupt and was auctioning everything off, including a huge pile of scrap iron the size of a three-bedroom house, which Dad bought. I was confused. What could we possibly do with that big pile of what looked like nothing? Dad had also purchased cutting torches and a backhoe and told me and Rocky to get to work hiring people to help us cut all the iron into three-foot pieces. In the meantime, Dad was going back to California to arrange for some trucks to haul it all back. He rented us a room down the road, and I remember telling him I was concerned we wouldn't have enough to eat, as we didn't have any money. When Rocky and I came back to the hotel that night after working all day, Dad had already left for California. But he had stocked our room with some milk and bread—and about forty cans of split pea soup. Because Dad didn't know how to read, he didn't know he had gotten all the same kind. But while it lacked variety, it kept us full.

About two days and four cans of soup later, I called my dad to tell him that we had found a lot of truck rear ends, bumpers, and transmissions in the pile and asked him what he wanted them to do with it all. Dad told us to put them aside, and a few days later he came to pick us all up and take us home—Rocky, me, the scrap iron, and the car parts.

I remember the city wasn't happy with my dad putting all this "junk" on a residential property, not to mention the big equipment he used to haul it. The rules were more lax back then but not that lax. Dad turned to the newspaper to solve that problem too, finding a small farm in Rio Linda to rent as his storage location. That helped the business grow even more. Scrap iron was seventeen dollars a ton, and back then Dad could buy cars for five dollars each off the street. If the car didn't have a radiator, he'd pay only three dollars a car. With Mom's help, he ran an ad in the *PennySaver* and started picking up nonfunctioning, abandoned cars every day.

Soon the farm became so full the county told Dad that he needed to get permits to continue doing business there. He sent me into town to get it done. At the time it cost just fifty dollars for the permit, and the only requirement was that we build a six-foot fence around the property, which we did right away, since I was already kind of a fence expert. It wouldn't be that easy these days, for sure.

We were now officially in the wrecking yard business. Dad would truck in the cars early in the morning. I was just shy of eighteen, and it was my job to flip the cars over on their sides with a boom truck and cut the motors out with cutting torches the way Dad had showed me. I'd then take a razor knife and cut the cotton out of the seats of the cars—a common filler for upholstery in vehicles made in the 1950s and 1960s. I'd put the cotton in burn piles and pull all the wire out of the car and put it into burn barrels, where I would burn the plastic off the wires to expose the copper underneath, which could then be sold to the smelter.

Many of the vehicle parts were made of pot metal, a cheaper type of metal that was used around tail lights and in grills. You could get money for pot metal too, so I would use a sledgehammer to separate it from the rest of the car. I'd also pull all the vehicles' starters and alternators for rebuilding. Each part that was valuable was separated out.

This was my introduction to the world of auto dismantling and recycling, and I loved it. I found enjoyment in the destruction—smashing and cutting and taking things apart. I didn't like putting cars together because it required too much precision. But it was easy to take cars apart. I also liked the idea that the cars were being reused in other ways. It was recycling in its earliest form.

There Comes a Time When You Have to Do It on Your Own

My dad had always been passionate about cars and was an avid Indianapolis 500 fan. But it wasn't until the wrecking yard that I really inherited his love of hot rods. It was there that I learned about different makes and models and began to pick out my favorites—including the short and muscular 1955 Chevy. Cars weren't just cars to me though. They also represented freedom. They helped me make money, but they also allowed me to get out of the house, chase girls, cruise with my friends, and frequent drive-ins like the Jolly Kone and A&W. With a car, it seemed like you could do anything.

My first real car that I purchased myself was a 1954 Ford that I bought for fifty dollars. I spent another ten dollars on about five cans of primer gray paint. I'd take that car to Lake Folsom, where I would frequently not just miss my curfew but ignore it altogether. I felt that since I was old enough to drive, I should do what I wanted to do. I never got into any real trouble, but I was getting tired of being under my father's thumb and wanted to do my own thing. I guess I was just a typical teenager in that I wanted more freedom and thought I was smarter than my parents.

It wasn't just me though. Dad had also changed. He had started drinking more, sipping on Jim Beam whiskey. When he drank, he'd get angry, and he and I would get into some epic arguments. Looking back on it, I think part of it is that my dad was just tired from working so hard for so long and frustrated that he always hit a roadblock because he couldn't read. Dad had always thought he was too old to go back to school or to learn to read. But that meant he had to rely on Mom and others to read for him—which made everything harder in a world that was already difficult to begin with.

So, for the first time, I started working for someone else other than my dad—Mr. Watson, who ran a chicken ranch. Mr. Watson was really easygoing and laid back, and I wasn't used to that. I shoveled chicken droppings from underneath the cages for extra money to pay for nights out on the town. With the work ethic I learned from my dad, I was a star employee.

After graduating from Rio Linda High School, I took another step toward independence and moved into my own place with Rocky. I didn't have a lot of dreams or ambition back then. I just wanted to continue to make money so I could have fun, race cars, and meet girls. But my plans would change six months later when I was drafted into the Vietnam War.

CHAPTER 2

Lessons the War Taught Me

> Every time you saw a soldier come around, it would take your breath away. You'd wonder if they were bringing news about your son.
>
> —Della Johnson

Find Something in Common to Unite Around

I learned I was going to Vietnam when Mom called me to say I had some mail at their house. I drove over to get it and opened up one letter, which said, "Your friends and neighbors have elected you to report to the United States Army ..."

I was confused. "Mom, what friends and neighbors would do this?" I asked her.

"It's a letter from the government, from Uncle Sam," Mom explained.

"Uncle Sam who?" I couldn't remember any uncle named Sam.

Finally Mom was able to get through to me that the president of the United States had drafted me into the military.

What Mom didn't tell me at the time was that she thought the military would be good for me and help me find my way. I was spending most of my time just having fun and wasn't too serious about anything—and she thought this might make me get serious.

But she was still concerned about Vietnam. She was careful not to show me, though. She didn't want to worry me. My dad got quiet when things bothered him, and he didn't say anything as I boarded the bus to basic training.

That bus was full of other long-haired eighteen-year-olds just like me. We laughed and smoked all the way there. We were nervous, but we hid that underneath jokes and banter. We were all strangers, but we were united by the shock of our lives.

First stop was the medical exam. We were told to strip down naked and then brought in groups before a doctor. I realized I had just gone from the freedom of my own apartment and a fast car to being the property of the United States Army.

Most of us passed the medical and were packed back onto the bus for Fort Ord. As we stepped off that bus, a man in a big brown hat started to yell at us. It sounded like he was going to beat us to death with words alone. He bellowed for us to line up, but we didn't have a notion what he expected, so that brought a whole lot more yelling and screaming. When we finally got into something like a line, we were sent one by one into a trailer. They set us down in that trailer and set to us with clippers that were hooked up to a vacuum. Buzz, buzz, buzz, and we were all shaved down. We went into that trailer hippies, frat guys, jocks, and nerds, but we came out the other end bald, shocked, and all looking a little ridiculous.

They fitted us all out with a duffel bag, socks, boots, T-shirts, and pants. By the time they finished filling up that bag, it probably outweighed me. Those fellas in the big brown hats kept yelling and we hauled … or drug … those duffels half a mile to the barracks, sweating from the heat and the strain.

At the barracks, we met our sergeant. That guy was meaner than anyone else we would come across during basic, and he wanted to make sure we knew it. He assigned each of us a bed, taught us how to make that bed, and then for a full day had us make and remake those beds till they were perfect. He promised us a cold drink and a chance to relax if the bed was perfect, but until then, we had to keep remaking it.

It took me a long time to figure out what was really going on. That sergeant wasn't all that concerned about the bed. He was just giving us something to unite around. That bed making brought us together. We all became buddies no matter where we had come from. It didn't matter if we were jocks or hippies. It was us against that sergeant. We all, every one, hated him.

But I tell you, I can still make a sharp bed.

Trust Your Gut and Keep Pressing Forward

We were pretty shook up. Our lives had changed suddenly, and every day was a new lesson, a new challenge, and usually a new insult from the sergeant. But I looked at it as an opportunity to learn. I knew if I could succeed, I could be a platoon leader. Maybe then I wouldn't have to do some of the grunt work the other soldiers did. So I worked hard, followed orders, and snapped to attention. All those years of working for my dad paid off. I was used to doing what needed to be done without hesitation.

After three months of grueling basic training, we took aptitude tests to figure out what we'd be doing for the army. Some of us were medics. Some were truck drivers. I ended up part of the infantry, learning how to tear down weapons and throw grenades.

I was part of the 1st Battalion, 16th Regiment, also known as 1/16th Rangers of The Big Red One.—an infantry unit with about 130 men in it. Every man in the unit earned a Purple Heart during my hitch. Only half survived.

My unit came in to help other units when they were already in the action. We'd sit on an airstrip with our packs and fly into hot landing zones (LZs) by helicopter to help secure the area and rescue soldiers who had been hit hard. If a plane went down, the unit would also be called in to secure the area around the wreckage and find the pilots.

We were the cavalry, basically. We didn't go in and stir up trouble; it was there when we got there. We just had to deal with it.

I started out as a fire direction center (FDC) because I was good with numbers. I used my math skills to determine where to set up guns and mortars for the first line of defense.

When the forward observer (FO) in the unit got killed, I got his job walking ahead of the company checking for ambushes and booby traps. It could be the most dangerous duty in the unit, and I learned to trust all my senses—including my gut—so I could warn the unit. If I didn't, then men behind me would be put at risk.

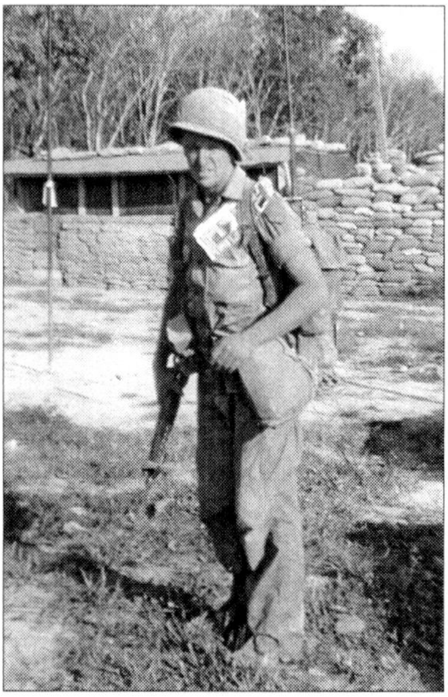

There was one ambush when the radio telephone operator (RTO) and I were cut off from the rest of the unit. Our instructions were to keep pressing forward, away from the unit, until we could be picked up. Well, I'll tell you it was difficult to resist the urge to turn back and help those guys under fire, but it was also terrifying to be cut off from the rest of the unit, alone and vulnerable. We were picked up by another unit, but that was tough. It wasn't the only time I was amazed at the army's persistence in protecting its soldiers. I was involved in a lot of fights where helicopters and troops would be sent in to rescue one or two men in similar situations, sparing no expense to save lives. It deepened my love for this country and my respect for the military.

While I was an FDC, I saw some pretty horrible things. If we found a village with Vietcong, we would surround it while an airplane dropped leaflets warning villagers they had twelve hours to get out before the area was bombed. Some would leave with their livestock. Others stayed as the village was destroyed by napalm. Sometimes enemy soldiers would break through, shooting mortars. Some would use villagers as human shields. Death was everywhere, and there were no rules for it.

When I was there, I didn't see many men break down because you had your buddies with you. After a big fire fight, the few who did start to break down could usually be brought back with the knowledge they had to take care of the wounded.

We'd slap them out of it and say, "Hey, get over there and help him; he's hurt." And as soon as they started working and helping someone else, the fear went away.

Push through the Fear

My Purple Heart came about eight months into my tour. My unit was in a hot LZ, called in to rescue another unit that had walked into a massive fort of Vietcong. As we flew in, the captain told us we would have to dig in deep because they would get hit hard that night. So we started to dig foxholes, using sandbags and trees as support.

It was really hot. I was lying at the top of the fox hole with my buddy Lamb. It was cooler up top. Suddenly we heard mortars coming in and folks yelling, "Mortars, mortars!" Lamb and I climbed down that hole as a mortar hit it from the top. I remember the *boom* of the mortar hitting, the ground shaking, and then dirt coming down on top of me as the foxhole caved in around us. Our faces and our guns were still out of the dirt, so we could shoot, but our bodies were buried up so we couldn't move. The whole side of the foxhole was gone, and more mortars were coming in. Shrapnel from the mortars was hitting the side of the foxhole, and I was sure we'd be overrun.

Miraculously, the fire stopped. When the unit dug me out, I was covered in blood and was pretty sure I was already dead. Turns out the blood was coming from one large wound and several smaller wounds around it. The sweat and flesh wounds made it seem much more serious than it was. After they hauled me away on a stretcher to the medic area, I was able to sit up. The corpsman came over to pack my wounds with gauze and tape them up. As he was working, they brought in a wounded enemy soldier. As the Cong was lying on the stretcher, he opened his hands, revealing a grenade ring on his finger. Everyone opened fired except for me. I'd lost my gun in the foxhole.

That night we patched up the wounded. We couldn't fly at night because we couldn't see the Vietcong soldiers, but the soldiers could sure see us. So we waited. I went out with the rest of the wounded and got more treatment for the mortar wounds. Then they sent me to base camp for a week to recover. In the Big Red One, you had to be wounded three times—or very badly—before you got to go home. I knew I was going back to the fight.

I didn't think twice about going into a foxhole again. Of course, I ended up digging shrapnel out of my arm and back over the next fifteen years as a result of the injuries. I guess there are just some things you have to do.

On one of the scariest nights I spent in Vietnam, my unit landed in another hot LZ in the middle of rice paddies. A river was running between where we had set up camp and where a group of men in our unit was going to set up an ambush. Lamb and I were supposed to set up a listening post outside the perimeter away from the main camp as an early-warning system against attack, with the river on one side and the rice paddies on the other.

Normally a listening post was within direct line of the camp, so if we heard anything, we could walk back into camp easily. But in this area, the river wasn't crossable. That meant we would have to follow the river to a crossing and then come back up to the camp. In essence, there was no going back. We were trapped over there.

The moon was bright that night as Lamb and I looked across the rice paddies, listening for the sound of enemy movement. Lamb suddenly whispered, "Do you hear something behind us?"

Well, that got my attention. I listened carefully. It sounded like Vietcong coming up the river. We radioed in to our lieutenant to warn the camp. He told us to throw grenades at the oncoming soldiers. If we threw the grenades down river, the camp would be too far away to be damaged by the explosions. But if the enemy got any closer and we were forced to shoot, we would be shooting across the river at our own unit. And the unit would be shooting at us.

We waited. We could hear them getting closer. When they got in range, we pulled the pins, threw the grenades, and got down. Those grenades landed near the river and shot up a spray of mud. Some of that mud hit guys in our unit, who pretty quickly yelled over the radio, "What are you guys doing?"

That was a long night. We'd listen for sounds, throw grenades, and get down. All night. But the Vietcong never made it to camp. Lamb and I were scared all night because we could hear them coming in, and we thought they'd get between us and camp. Then we'd be trapped. I have probably had more dreams about that night than the night I got wounded. I probably woke up in a sweat more over that night than any others over the years. I guess it's because we couldn't see them, but we knew they were there. And we knew we couldn't shoot, or we might shoot our own guys. So if the enemy got to us, we were caught. That was a long, long night.

Life Is Precious. Make It Count.

Two months after that long night on the river, Lamb was killed in an ambush. He was twenty-four, a coach at a junior high school. He was just one of tens of thousands of guys who died over there and one of many friends I would lose.

I also lost my best friend, David Flower, to the war. David had joined up rather than being drafted. Since he'd enlisted, he had more choice of what he did in the war. He started out as a cook, and after I was drafted, we exchanged letters. Our friend Ivy Burgess was also in the infantry, though in a different unit than I was. We talked about starting a business together after the war. It was the dream young men have when they have a new appreciation for having a life ahead of them.

David would get letters about all the fighting Ivy and I were involved in, but since he was a cook, he didn't see any action himself. So at the end of his tour, he extended and came back as a chopper gunner. He wanted to serve his country, and he wanted to do it fighting, not cooking. David's older brother also served in the military, and there was a rule at the time that only one brother could be in a war zone at a time. David told me he extended his duty to save his brother from having to fight and possibly get killed. It was the ultimate sacrifice.

Mom broke the news of David's death to me. He was long buried by the time I got home. The war was hard on me, but it was also hard on Mom. She said that every time she saw a soldier come around, it would take her breath away. She'd wonder if they were bringing news about me. My brother Curtis told me later that every night she would watch the news for updates on the war. She would pray every day and trusted that God would bring me home safe. Now, she didn't believe in asking God for things. She just trusted him. But Curtis tells me she prayed every night and worried every day.

I called home while I was on R and R once. I was just so happy to be away from the fighting with my buddies and able to have a little fun. When we had to go back to the fighting, I called again. I don't think I could keep the tears out of my voice. It was hard. And it was hard on the families at home too.

Your Decisions Impact Others

In the late summer of 1967, one year after I went to Vietnam, I had finally fought enough. I boarded a plane with a group of soldiers, and they took us home. The soldiers were dead quiet as the plane took off, and they remained that way until the pilot told us we were out of gun range and safe. Well, that's when the hollering and celebrating started. We threw our hats up in the air, and I realized we had all been tensed up at the last moment, convinced we'd be shot down. But we were finally free. Nothing could hurt us anymore. That was the greatest relief any of us would ever feel.

The war gave me a new sense of purpose, and it taught me a lot I'd apply to the business world later. The military instilled responsibility in me. As an FDC, the unit relied on my decision about where to set up the guns and where to shoot. And when I was a forward observer, the weight of anybody getting past us was on my shoulders. I realized how important my decisions were—how they could impact other people. Later, when I got into business, I better understood my responsibility as an employer. I was giving people the means to buy their own homes or send their kids to college. In the war, if you made the wrong decision, people died. But if you don't take care of your company, people lose their jobs and their livelihoods. So the war taught me how to make the best decisions for the people around me, not just for myself.

And the military taught me other lessons too. Having good leaders and a clear chain of command is important. And it taught me cleanliness and order. Keeping things lined up makes for efficiency. In the military, we were told to face right and line everything up from shoulder to nose. I brought that back to the dismantling business, lining up the cars in the yard in a perfect row. I also learned that a coat of paint helped cover up a lot of bad stuff and was the cheapest way to make something bad look good.

In basic training, I remember staying up all night to buff the barracks floor for the next morning's inspection. If we didn't pass or the beds weren't made properly, we wouldn't get a weekend. So, if we finished the floor early, we'd walk in our sock feet and sleep on top of our made bunks to make sure we didn't scuff or mess up anything. The military teaches you order, timing, and discipline. It teaches you how to work as a team. It was the best education I could get.

I didn't talk about Vietnam for more than twenty years after I got back. Then I visited the Vietnam Veterans Memorial in Washington, DC. I went down there looking for David's name, as well as other friends I'd lost. I found one name before I started to have a panic attack. I ran up the hill out of that memorial and never went back.

It was like a dark cloud that came over the top of me, and I was suffocating. There were just too many ghosts and bodies and people there. You could see all the names, and it was overwhelming. It's probably the best memorial ever made. But now I know why veterans go down there and cry. It has an unbelievable power.

I realized then that you can't go through something like Vietnam and bury it forever. So I started to talk about it, and eventually I found peace after years of ignoring that time.

Willis Johnson

I guess I was a different kind of soldier, because when I got home, I just wiped it out of my head. Even though I came back with a Purple Heart and a Metal of Merit for Heroism, along with other citations, I put them in a drawer instead of showing them off.

I was done. I didn't watch the news. I served my time, and it was over. But I had buddies who lived it over and over. They talked about it, and they hung around each other. They couldn't let it go. I disassociated myself from them because I didn't want to talk about it.

I wanted the war in the past. Behind me. I came back determined to be successful. My sister Bonnie says I really grew up in Vietnam. I told my sister Lequeita that I was going to come home, get married, and become a millionaire. And that's what I did.

CHAPTER 3

Lessons I Learned While Starting a Family

> Sometimes things happen to you that you look back on and know that it was the most important decision of your life.
>
> —Joyce (Cox) Johnson

If You Snooze, You Lose—in Love and in Business

I was home from Vietnam for a short time before I had to go to Fort Benning, Georgia, to serve out my last six months in the army. I'd found that the best way to forget about Vietnam was to pick up where I left off—being around my buddies, driving cars, dancing, and hanging out at the drive-in. Everybody figured out their own way to deal with it, and that was mine.

I was at a basketball game at my former high school when I tripped over a young woman's legs. And she wasn't too happy about it.

I remember her saying, "Hey! Watch where you're going!"

I thought, *Geez, I'm sorry. It's no big deal.*

A few days later, Glenn Cunningham and I heard about a Halloween party my sister Aliece was throwing. It sounded like a good way to meet some girls, drink a little, dance, and have some fun. My other sister, Bonnie, had invited her friend Joyce Cox to attend the same party and had told her she wanted her to meet her brother, who just got back from the war. Maybe they could date, she suggested.

Joyce told her, "Okay, as long as he doesn't want to get serious."

Glenn had also just returned from Vietnam, where he had lost one of his fingers. Glenn started dancing with one of the girls at the party, and I asked him who she was. I had an interest since she was the same girl whose legs I had tripped over the day before.

Glenn told me her name was Joyce Cox and that he had asked her out. She had told him to give her a call.

Well then I stepped right up and asked Joyce to dance and also asked her out while I was at it. I got the same response: "Well, give me a call."

I didn't hesitate. The next day, I called Joyce and asked her out.

It's just like in business; you don't want to wait too long or you might lose the deal.

Joyce said she didn't know when she'd be able to see me. She had a small baby girl, Reba, from a prior marriage that had been annulled. Joyce had to take Reba to the doctor that day.

"Well, I can take you and the baby to the doctor," I offered.

Joyce tells me suddenly she knew I was different. She liked the way I included Reba and the way I spelled things out about what I wanted, and she felt secure with that. Joyce gave me her address—which was on Willis Avenue.

"Well this is an omen," I told her, and we laughed about it for a bit.

As I drove down Willis Avenue later that day, I saw a beautiful woman all dressed up with her hair done and makeup on waiting outside. I thought she was the prettiest woman I'd ever seen. And I drove right by.

I didn't recognize it as being Joyce. I got to the end of the street and had to turn around before realizing the mistake. We took Reba to the doctor, and then I took them out to Sam's Hoffbrau, where we ate and visited for hours.

Joyce, who lived with her parents, made arrangements for them to babysit, and the two of us went out again that night. And again the next night. We were rarely apart.

On one of our dates, I told Joyce one day I would be rich. She didn't have any reason to believe me. I wasn't showing any signs of that at the time. But she liked that I had ambition. She liked that I had plans. Not just for the evening—plans for everything.

It was ten days after our first date when I came over to her house to fill her in on more of my plan. It was Joyce's birthday, and I had recruited Aliece to help me pick out a present for her—an engagement ring.

See, I was about to go to Fort Benning to complete my military duty and wanted Joyce to come with me. But Joyce had made it clear she wasn't going anywhere unless she was married.

So I figured I'd solve that problem. It just seemed like the thing to do. I wanted to be with her, and this was the way to make it happen.

She hadn't been expecting me to come over until later that day. We had plans for dinner. But I couldn't wait. Bonnie and I came by earlier—and Joyce still had her hair in curlers. I sat her down in the front seat of my car and told her there was a present for her in the glove box.

She was shocked. I'd talked about marriage, but she didn't know I was serious. But that's just the way I am. I knew what I wanted, and I wanted to get settled down and build a life. People think it's funny that I asked her after such a short period of time. I think it's funny she said yes.

Joyce says it wasn't funny at all.

She says that sometimes things happen to you that you look back on and know that it was the most important decision of your life. At that time you just know it's the right way to go. It's like a gut feeling or knowing what they mean when they say soul mates.

From the moment we met, Joyce knew I was confidant and determined. She liked that. She might have thought I was kind of cute too.

I had dated girls before, and Joyce had been married. And neither of us had really had plans for things to happen so fast. But the two of us just clicked in a way I knew I wasn't going to find anywhere else. She was interested in everything I talked about and wanted to hear what she had to say as well. She knew my sisters and liked cars so much she even knew all the makes and models. Both our families were from Oklahoma and Arkansas and had similar beliefs and work ethics.

The fact that I was also getting a daughter in the package made it an even better deal.

I was raised with five sisters, so being around a baby wasn't anything out of the ordinary. And I was in love with Joyce, so I was in love with the baby. Reba was part of Joyce.

I had to report to Fort Benning, Georgia, shortly after Thanksgiving to complete my time in the service. Joyce and I corresponded and talked about getting married when I got out of the army in April. But when I came home on Christmas Eve, we decided we couldn't wait. We drove to Carson City, Nevada, on Christmas Day and got married on December 26, 1968. I was twenty-one and Joyce twenty.

When Times Get Tough, Get Creative

I was just finishing up my military service when Joyce and I were married. She and Reba took the train to meet me at Fort Benning, and we lived just off base in a small town called Columbus. I was a SPEC 5 (Specialist) making about $140 a month, about $42 more than I would if I was single, so we couldn't afford our own car. But our house had a big field behind it, so I offered to have GIs park their vehicles out there. Cars that weren't insured weren't allowed on base, and at the time cars didn't have to be insured by law. Servicemen often didn't have the money to get insurance, so they parked their vehicles off base. In exchange for storing their car at my house, I was able to borrow the vehicle if I needed it. There were always two or three cars to choose from and even a motorcycle now and then. It was my own little rental agency. And it saved me money we couldn't afford to spend on a car.

Don't Be Afraid to Get Dirty

I always kind of expected that when my service to my country was done, I'd go back to work for my dad in California at the dismantling yard. And that's exactly what I did, at least for a while. And even after everything I'd already learned growing up and in the war, Dad still had things to teach me.

Dad had learned—again through the newspaper—that a wrecking yard called Red's Auto Wrecking was auctioning off its inventory in Weed, California. We hopped in the truck to go look at the yard, which was filled with thousands of old cars, including Packards, Henry Js, Kaiser-Frazers, Chevys, and Fords. The wrecking yard was old too. The motors were out of some of the cars, and there was a tree about six inches in diameter growing through one car. Dad told me to take a piece of paper and inventory every car in the yard—marking down if was 50 percent there, 75 percent there, or all there; if it had a motor; and its size. I crawled through every square inch of that place, climbing through snake-filled weeds with a can of paint I used to mark the cars so I knew which ones I already had done.

Meanwhile, Dad was estimating scrap tonnage and trying to figure out how he'd move it all if he bought it. I had read to him the guidelines for the auction, which included the highest bidder having to clear all the cars in ninety days or pay a penalty. That didn't leave much time to separate the usable parts and haul the metal to a smelter.

At the hotel that night, Dad went over my inventory numbers and did his final calculation, thinking out loud as he did so. He'd tell me which cars had the most metal and how much we could get for radiators and other parts. It was another education in recycling.

But it would also prove to be an education in the bidding system. The next day, we went into a big room with a big table where businessmen with diamond rings, expensive watches, and cowboy hats were prepared to bid against us. They all looked polished and pristine, while we still had the dirt from the wrecking yard on us from crawling through cars the day before.

It was a sealed bid auction. Dad wrote his bid down silently on a piece of paper and put it in an envelope, not even showing it to me first. All the envelopes went to the center of the table and were opened up one at a time. One bid was $12,000, another $13,000. Dad's bid was $15,000; he had won.

I was excited. There was a lot of work to do, but it was going to be cool, I thought. We were going to be sittin' in high cotton with all these cars! Then, as we walked out of the room, one of the businessmen approached us and offered $5,000 for us to walk away and let him take over the note for the $15,000 bidding price. Dad refused.

I couldn't believe it. At the time, you could buy a three-bedroom home for around $8,000. Dad was being offered a lot of profit for doing nothing. How could he turn that down?

"He'll go to the hotel and think about it, and he'll come back tomorrow with more money," Dad reassured me. "In the meantime, there are guys out here who still want stuff."

Sure enough, thirty minutes later another man approached us from Harrah's car collection in Reno. He told us he wanted to buy and restore fifteen cars at the yard, so the three of us went to check them out. Dad made a deal with the buyer from Harrah's to purchase the fifteen cars for $5,000 but told him he'd have to get the cars off the land within the week.

There were still about two thousand cars left, and it was then I started understanding just how lucrative the yard could be. The cotton had just gotten a lot higher.

It got even higher when the first businessman approached us the next day with a better deal—$10,000 if we walked away and he took over the note.

Dad told the businessman he would do the deal if he could take fifteen cars of his choice for Harrah's and if the businessman would sign 100 percent liability for the deal. He also had one other condition—the businessman would have to have all the cars off the property in seventy days, or Dad would get the entire yard back and finish cleaning it up without having to pay any penalties if it wasn't done by the ninety-day deadline.

The businessman agreed, and Dad walked away with $15,000 without having to do any work. It was in that moment I thought Dad was the best negotiator in the world.

I also learned another important lesson that day. The reason we were able to make such a good deal was because we were the only guys who got dirty. We did our homework and knew exactly what we were buying. As a result, Dad was able to outbid the others, who didn't know the true value of the yard or had underestimated what others knew about its value.

It was also another example of why it's important to take action and not procrastinate. The announcement about the yard being for sale was in the newspaper on Friday. We drove there on Saturday, walked the yard on Sunday, and placed the bid Monday. If we had hesitated, we would not have been able to make the deal.

Into Each Life a Little Snow Must Fall, but You Don't Have to Like It

Although I was still learning from my dad, something was missing. Joyce and I were also craving our independence as newlyweds and wanted to be more on our own. I think there were just too many people who were involved in our lives from both sides of our families, and we needed to be by ourselves.

I also had big ideas to innovate Dad's yard and was trying to get him to make changes. But Dad was more conservative than I was. While Dad was a gambler in a lot of ways, he didn't want to gamble with what he already had.

My sister Lequeita thought I would really be able to help Dad grow the business. But Dad just didn't trust me. He was an old-school wrecker, and my ideas were very new.

So when a friend who was in a wheelchair purchased a farm in Deer Park near Spokane, Washington, I offered to help him move and get the farm up and running if we could live on the ranch for a while. Joyce and I loaded up a big truck with all our belongings and moved everything to Washington state.

After helping with the farm, I found a job at a logging mill, and Joyce went to work as a nurses' aide at a hospital. But the logging mill would have frequent shutdowns, meaning I couldn't count on a steady paycheck.

Then there was the snow, which began to fall in October and by Thanksgiving was piled high. Reba's earliest memories are of that winter. She was afraid of the snow and thought it would swallow her up. I helped convince her that wouldn't happen, and she faced her fear.

But while the snow didn't swallow any of us whole, it did take its toll on us. We were struggling, barely able to keep a roof over our heads and beans and pasta on the table. Every paycheck went to the local store to pay for food and fuel.

It was what we had wanted, though. We were making it on our own, even if it was by the skin of our teeth.

Joyce says we really came together during this time. We became a team and learned a lot about survival. We had to. We didn't have a safety net—just each other.

Look Out for Dishonest People

We finally caught a break when I was offered a job at a Safeway store in Spokane. By April, we were expecting a baby.

Everyone who worked at Safeway seemed to be going to college, and the store supported scheduling around classes. I decided maybe I should take advantage of the GI bill and take classes too, and I enrolled in community college.

I didn't stay in school long, though. It just wasn't for me. I already knew the math they were teaching after years of using it in both business and the military. Basically I wasn't learning anything new about the things I was interested in and was wasting my time taking classes I wasn't interested in like sociology. I didn't want to analyze people. So after one semester of that, I decided to drop out.

Instead, I got more shifts at Safeway, where I was learning more practical business skills like balancing cash registers, ordering, security, and loss prevention. As Safeway operated on a very slim profit margin, my dad's advice to "take care of your pennies and the dollars will take care of themselves" came in handy once again. If employees didn't account for every penny, the store might not succeed.

All of us would take our lunch breaks in a room above the store. This was before stores commonly installed security cameras, so the room was also a great way to observe customers and catch them stealing.

Boy, was that an eye opener. I found out just how dishonest people could really be sitting above that store. That little old lady that you never thought would steal was putting stuff in her purse when no one was looking, or the fat guy was putting pork ribs down his pants and walking out of the store. It made me really think of how theft can affect a business and how you can't ignore it.

Safeway also reinforced the need for order that was established earlier when I was in the army. The aisles had to be organized and clean for people to want to shop and so they could find what they were looking for. That meant paying attention to stock empty shelves, checking expiration dates, and holding specials for items that were overstocked.

Don't Trust Unions

Safeway was also a good role model for taking care of its employees. Not only did they accommodate their employees who wanted to go to college, but they also took special steps to ensure employee safety. I liked that and wanted to be the same kind of employer.

Safeway was unionized, but that wasn't the reason they treated their employees so well. In fact, the experience I had with the union at Safeway left me suspicious of unions for the rest of my life. While I was there, Safeway had offered a series of raises to its employees over a three-year contract. All the employees were called in to the union hall to vote on the offer, and it passed by an overwhelming majority. A few weeks later, however, the union had another vote and only invited those they knew would vote against the offer. The vote failed, resulting in a strike.

It was a trick vote, and that's when I realized how unions operate. Safeway had been good to us, working around our school schedules and teaching us about the business, and everyone at our store was very upset about having to strike because they liked working there. But the union didn't care about that.

I refused to carry a picket sign and instead supplemented my income during the strike by shoveling snow. But strike aside, I realized Joyce and I were not really happy in Washington state, and we definitely weren't looking forward to another winter there either. Joyce was especially missing home and really wanted to be close to her mother when she had the baby.

A short time after the strike started, I was talking to my dad on the phone during my lunch hour about how things weren't going as well as I liked. Dad offered me another opportunity to come back and work for him. He also offered me something he never had before—part ownership in the company. He promised me that if I worked at the dismantling yard, I would get 10 percent of the business and the profits. Granted, I wouldn't be earning that much—just $1.10 an hour—but I'd also get commission for the sales I made.

Once again I didn't hesitate to make a decision, and I jumped on my dad's offer. That's how I earned a reputation as a gunslinger, I guess. You can't hesitate when you are in a gunfight either, or you won't see another one. I called my manager and told him I quit because I didn't like what the union was doing and to send my check to my parents' address in California. Then I rented a moving truck, packed up the house again, and started to make the journey back to Rio Linda with Joyce and Reba that very night.

When You Make a Promise to Someone, Keep It

Back home and back at the business I loved, I took all I had learned in the military and at Safeway and applied it to dismantling. I tripled the income at the yard by taking good care of customers and calling body shops and mechanics to tell them what inventory we had in stock. I was buying more scrap cars, scrapping more cars, and pushing more iron and parts through. I even hired more people to keep up with the demand—something Dad never wanted to do because that meant having to read and fill out paperwork.

Dad had been slowing down at the business as well, which opened the door even wider for me to do what I wanted to do. He was getting ready to retire and was taking more trips in his camping trailer with Mom, leaving the day-to-day business duties to me. But there was a part of Dad I think that also didn't know what to do without the business and wasn't ready to fully let it go.

When all my hard work earned me a huge commission check, Dad asked me to let it ride so the money could go back into the business instead. He offered me the use of the company truck instead and again promised me a percentage of the business as it grew.

I agreed to put the money back into the business because I knew from what my dad had taught me that was the right thing to do. And I continued to run the company like it was mine because I thought a portion of it was. I expanded the business to a large dairy farm next door and got it zoned so they could rent out some of the land to other local dismantlers. Customers going to the other dismantlers would have to drive by our yard first, which led to more business. I would also purchase parts from the other dismantlers and turn them for a profit. Dad didn't like this at all. He didn't want me helping his competitors make money—even if it meant we made more money.

Dad was angry a lot during this time, and a lot of it had to do with the fact he was drinking. When Dad drank, his temper would run even shorter, and then he and I would argue about the best direction for the business. In fact, we rarely agreed on anything anymore.

Finally, it was my turn to take a vacation and leave the business in Dad's hands for a while. I asked Dad if I could borrow $500 from the business to travel to Arkansas with Joyce and visit her parents, who were now living there. Dad said the business couldn't afford to loan me the money, so I went to the bank to get a loan instead. At the time I didn't mind. Again, the business comes first.

A short time after I got back, though, my uncle and aunt came to California from Oklahoma to visit while on their vacation. Dad told me to write them a check from the business for $500 as he had promised to pay for their vacation if they came to visit. I was furious and told him to write the check himself.

Dad couldn't understand why I was upset. "It's my money," he told me.

Well that just irritated me even more.

"Ten percent of it is mine," I reminded him. "And if you aren't paying for my vacation, you aren't paying for his."

I stormed off, leaving Dad to do what he liked and close the business up himself. The next day I came back, but we were no less mad at each other. Dad had also been drinking whiskey, which made things even worse. He'd had a fight with my brother Curtis that day too. In the end, we all decided to go our separate ways.

That was hard. I had always admired my dad, but I was also hurt and disappointed. But I learned a valuable lesson; when you make a promise to someone, you better keep it. After Dad backed out of the promise he made me, I told myself I would never do that, even if it meant I would lose money. I never promised something to someone that I didn't do, and I never made promises I couldn't keep. My word is gold. You don't have to get me to sign something for me to take my commitment seriously. That was a really good lesson to learn, even if there were better ways to learn it.

You Need to Sacrifice to Build a Dream

I used my experience at Safeway to get a job at another grocery chain—Raley's Bel Air—while Curtis got a job at Teichert Construction. I was a floater, working a week at one store and another week at a different store, filling in at various positions, from assistant manager to produce manager to ordering manager. I enjoyed it because I got to do something different all the time and continued to learn about retail.

I also used my GI benefits to help purchase a home for my growing family, which now included my younger daughter, Tammi. The house had cost eleven thousand dollars, and the payment was ninety-nine dollars a month. Money was tight.

I didn't know how I was going to handle it. I remember sitting down to figure out how many diapers we had to wash in the coin machines and whether we would be better off to go to Sears and buy a washer and pay it off for ten dollars a month.

Then I injured my collarbone and couldn't work for a short period of time. Joyce was cleaning houses and selling Tupperware, and I sold my motorcycle and truck to help us all scrape by.

Although times were hard, I never stopped dreaming big and looking for something better. I wanted more for my family, and I knew the only way to do that was to put fate in my own hands and start my own business.

Also, like my dad, I just couldn't shake my love of the dismantling business. After about nine months at Raley's, I took some time off to try to find a wrecking yard to invest in. I knew we had already earned some equity in our house, and my plan was to use that equity to buy a dismantling yard of my own.

Joyce's brother, Terry, and I had talked about getting a yard in Oklahoma—where land was cheaper. We even drove there for two weeks with the goal of finding a yard. But Joyce did not want to go back to Oklahoma. She had made a home in California and wanted to stay. So she called on a valuable ally. She prayed that we not find a yard in Oklahoma. She trusted God to help and believed there had to be a yard in California we could buy instead. God listened.

I never could beat my wife's prayers, and I never did find a yard in Oklahoma. But when I came home in August of 1972, I did find a little five-acre auto-dismantling yard in Rancho Cordova called Rand's Auto Wreckers. The owners were in their sixties and ready to retire, so I asked them if they wanted to sell. They told me they did, and set their price at $75,000.

Well, that was a lot of money in those days. I mean, we had just bought a 1,600-square-foot, three-bedroom home for around $11,000. I didn't have a lot of money saved up either, but like my dad, I knew how to make a deal.

I offered them $15,000 down with interest-only payments, with the rest of the money due in five years. They agreed.

There was just one more problem. I didn't have $15,000. That took more dealing. I figured I could borrow $5,000. I already had $5,000. That left me needing just $5,000 more to close the deal. So I went home and told Joyce we would have to sell our house.

Joyce was concerned at first. "Where are we going to live?" she asked me.

"Well, you know there is a little trailer out at the wrecking yard that is twelve feet wide and about thirty feet long. Me, you, and the kids can live there, and I can work until midnight if I have to," I told her.

You know, Dad and I are probably the two luckiest men alive. We both married women who believed in us and were willing to sacrifice while we chased our dreams. Joyce agreed to sell the house, pack up the kids, and move again.

I still needed a little more money, however. I took a loan from the bank, as did Curtis, who agreed to partner with me. Joyce's parents, as well as her sister and brother-in-law, also took out loans to give to me. Terry, Joyce's brother, pitched in too. Joyce's other sister and brother-in-law also lent them the money they had saved for taxes.

I was very lucky so many people believed in me. Our families were all very close and supportive, and they wanted to help us. Joyce remembers being excited because we were starting something that was truly ours. We had help, but it was ours.

When the deal was done, Joyce and I stood at all four corners of the yard and dedicated the business to the Lord. It was the beginning of a tradition that would carry out through the rest of our lives.

Ideas Can Come from Anywhere—Even John Wayne

After signing the paperwork and praying, it was time to get to work. Curtis and I changed the name to Mather Auto Dismantlers after the nearby air force vase. But it was truly a junkyard, at least at the beginning. Joyce called it a shack, and I guess she was pretty much right. There were piles of junk, dog food cans, beer cans … it was a mess.

But it was our mess. And it was all we could afford. I was twenty-six, and I had big plans for that little yard.

By this time my son Jason had been born, coming shortly after Tammi. We moved from our spacious home to the tiny trailer, with two tiny bedrooms and one tiny bathroom. The planes from the air base would make the windows shake, but that wasn't the worst part about it, at least for Joyce.

The first night we stayed there, you could hear the mice crawling around and chewing on the walls. Joyce doesn't like mice.

For those of you not in the business, a dismantling yard primarily deals in used auto parts and recycling scrap iron. I would buy cars—mostly the ones that weren't drivable and had come to the end of their life—and pay thirty-five dollars to fifty dollars and then tow them to the yard. There, I'd pull all the parts off that I thought I could resell, drain the fluids out of the car (which is called "depolluting"), and then haul the shell to the smelter, where I'd get paid for the iron by the ton. If I had a motor that was cast iron, or any copper or aluminum, I got paid different rates for that as well.

At first, when I didn't have a lot of money, I relied on the scrap iron to make ends meet. As the business grew, I hoped to be able to buy better cars and build up the parts side of the business.

I used an old portable building on the property as an office. A Quonset hut also sat on the property, full of leftover junk from the previous owners of the yard. I used the Quonset hut to cut up cars.

One rare night, though, I was in the trailer watching an old John Wayne movie about World War II. In the movie, John Wayne kicked down the doors of a Quonset hut that housed the officer's club. The movie made me think of my own prefabricated, semicircular steel hut in a new light.

I thought, *Well, if they can make it look decent in the movie, decorate it all up for officers, maybe I can do that.*

I started moving all the leftover junk out of the hut. Then I bought new paneling that I screwed into the walls to make it look more like a permanent structure. Finally, I poured a new concrete slab and installed a new door.

In two weeks we had a bigger, better Mather store—and it was all thanks to John Wayne!

Find a Way to Balance Business and Family

It was a unique experience living at a wrecking yard. My kids hated getting picked up by the bus because the other kids would make fun of them when they saw they lived in a scrapyard. The girls were often teased and called "Junkyard Annies."

But it wasn't all bad. The yard was also a great place for kids with imaginations. Jason played hide and seek, cowboys and Indians, tag, and other games among the piles of wrecked cars. It was definitely a boy's idea of the perfect playground. As a toddler, Jason would collect Hot Wheels cars and pretend he had his own dismantling yard, smashing the most undesirable cars with a hammer to wreck them. I have to admit that kind of made me smile.

Mather was truly a family business. I would bring in cars and parts, while Curtis called around to body shops and other dismantlers to sell what I had brought in. Joyce helped with DMV work, while the kids would take off license plates or clean out the cars when they got to the yard, collecting leftover cans for money.

Tammi says she and the other kids all learned how to work and about the value of work during that time. She also says I set a good example for them about how to work hard. But really, I was just doing what I had to do—working late nights and weekends to make the business work.

I did make a point, however, of reserving Sundays for family. I drove a big international school bus from the yard around Mather Air Force Base to pick up children and take them to Sunday school. Jason, who was about four or five, would go with me and sit on the heater box for the route. Joyce and the girls would meet us at the church, where she taught Sunday school. I would stay for the service and then repeat my bus route before going back to the yard. Then all of us would go together to another service in the evening.

While I was building the company, that was our time because building a successful business means nothing if you don't have your family or your faith.

I did try to use the business to teach my kids some important lessons. Reba tells me I never expected anything from anyone that I wouldn't do myself, and she's right. I used to dismantle cars alongside my employees. The joke was that I permanently had grease under my nails. I even rebuilt an old '59 Ford tow truck from parts I found in the yard so I could tow vehicles.

With the tow truck now functional, I could go out and purchase cars for between ten dollars and thirty dollars and bring them back to the yard. A crew there would take the parts off that I marked to sell and cut the rest up for scrap. Then they'd load the scrap cars onto a big truck, which I would drive to Niles Canyon near Union City at four in the morning to get in line so I could sell the iron for cash. I would go early enough so I could get back and pick up more cars during the day.

Jason would often go with me. I would get him out of bed at four in the morning and carry him to a pallet on the floorboard of the truck, where he could sleep. Halfway, I would stop for breakfast. Jason would wake up to eat and talk and then fall asleep again for the rest of the trip. He'd then wake up again to watch the scrap cars be unloaded. It was a fun time for us both, and I got to teach Jason about cars, which he's always been passionate about. He would also go with me on buying trips to auctions in Reno, where I would explain why I was bidding on certain cars and how much they were worth.

I guess Jason wanted to be around me, just like I wanted to be around my dad at that age.

On one such trip to Union City to sell scrap iron, I struck up a conversation with Jimmy Meeks, who worked for his dad who had a yard in the Bay Area. Jimmy and I would drink coffee and talk shop. We recognized in each other a common passion for the business, a strong work ethic, and a high standard of fairness that would later cause our paths to become permanently intertwined.

I would repeat this early-morning ritual of driving to Union City three to four days a week. I needed every extra penny coming in so I could put it back into the business and keep it going.

I was so anxious to work for myself that I didn't think it was tough. But Joyce remembers going to the bank sometimes twice a day to cover the checks. The bank was way across town, but someone had to make the trip. Still, Joyce admits it was a fun time because I was able to build my dream—and the whole family had a hand in that.

My nephew, Rick Harris, worked as a young boy at Mather breaking down tires for a nickel apiece. Rick remembers that I drove a beat-up Oldsmobile with a big dent on the side because I couldn't afford anything better. All my extra money was going to the business. To be honest, I got stranded more than once in the car, but luckily I was mechanically inclined and could fix it most of the time. It was just a sacrifice I was willing to make.

Thank goodness my wife was also willing to sacrifice and supported me. We lived on a budget, and if we didn't have the money, we just didn't have the money and wouldn't do it. We didn't go out to eat or to the movies. We lived to get the business going. Joyce told me later that she always knew all of those sacrifices would be worth it one day.

She was right, and Mather proved to be the mother business for many successful businesses to come.

CHAPTER 4

Lessons I Learned Building a Dream

> I'm going to Detroit to see Mr. Iacocca, and I am going to make some money.
>
> —Willis Johnson, referring to Lee Iacocca, president of Chrysler.

The Sum of Parts Is Greater Than the Whole—at Least in Dismantling

Mather may have started as a shack, but it soon took off thanks in part to Curtis' sales skills and a lot of hard work. My dream to build up the parts side of the business was starting to come true. As I was able to buy better cars, Mather was able to stock more and better parts, including motors, transmissions, and rear ends. As this happened, the business relied less on scrap iron, which gradually went from the main revenue stream to a byproduct of the parts business. The better the cars I could buy, the better the parts, and the better the profits. We were also able to pay off all the money friends and family gave us to start the business.

One other big boost was that I was the first in the industry to dismantle parts, not just cars. Typically, if someone came into a dismantling shop and asked for a 4.6 liter motor, the shop would pull the whole motor out of a wrecked car and sell the motor and everything hanging on it—including the alternator, starter, regulator, smog pumps, air breather, carburetor, and distributor. A fully dressed 318 Dodge engine with twenty-two thousand miles on it might have cost a customer about $400 back in the early '70s and would have come with a warranty.

But if the motor had been sitting for a while, the carburetor might be dried out—the water pump shot or other parts didn't fit the car just right—meaning there was a good chance the dismantler would have to buy it back to honor the warranty. The customer might also already have a good alternator and not need another one. But they were forced to buy the whole package. That didn't make sense to me.

That's why if the same customer went into Mather, he or she would find just the motor—steam cleaned and painted and looking brand-new. The additional parts would have been taken out as soon as the motor had arrived to the yard, restored, and sold separately so customers could buy only what they needed.

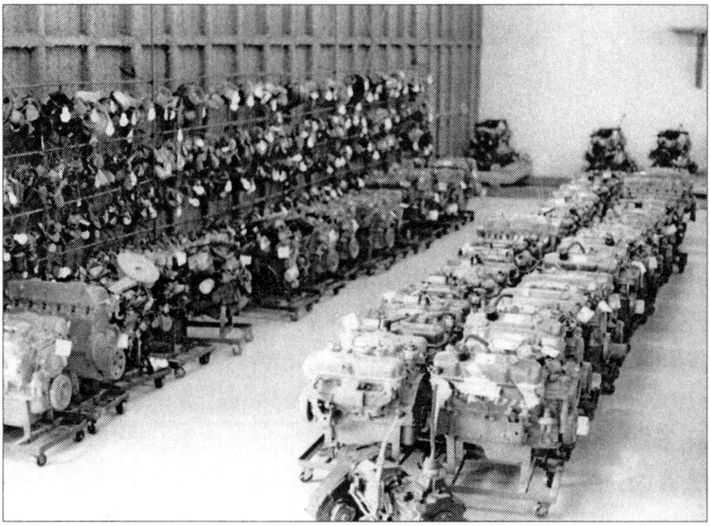

I would sell them just the motor, undressed, for $275—a deal if that's all they needed. Then I'd sell the other parts separately—the distributor for $50, the alternator for $25, the carburetor for $100. By the time I was done, I could get $700 for the same parts sold separately that were sold together by my competitor for $400. And the customer was happier. I also had fewer buy-backs because I didn't have to guarantee all the parts on the motor. This caused my profit margins to far exceed that of my competitors.

Unlike other wrecking yards, I also held sales and theme days, like Western Day, to bring in customers. It was something I learned from my time in the grocery business. I would also paint the floors every year to make the shop look clean and organize parts neatly in racks by type, which saved the customers time and allowed them to compare. Each part was also cleaned, because I knew customers would pay more for them if they looked like they were fresh out of a box.

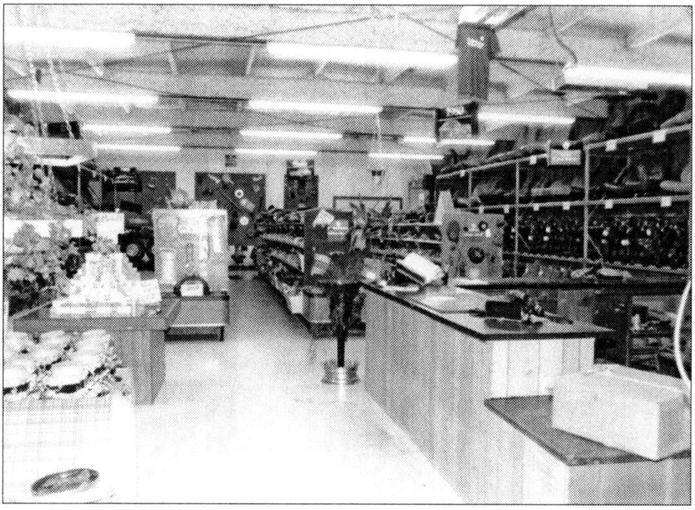

Whatever made it look nice, we did. That way, when people walked in, it was like they were walking into a real retail store. It made it more personal. They could shop. I know that sounds crazy—shopping at a wrecking yard. But no matter what you are buying, you want it to be a good experience, and you want to find what you want easily. Up until then, people just thought of a wrecking yard as a bunch of wrecked cars in a field that you had to wander through to find what you wanted. But we changed that. They didn't even have to look at a car. They could find what they wanted on the shelf.

Life Is Fragile, So Make the Best of It

As sales and inventory grew, I needed a bigger building to display all the parts and to continue to grow. Just like my dad, I turned to the paper for a solution. I saw a metal building for sale in West Sacramento, a fabricated four-thousand-square-foot building that had been put up to serve as a Seventh Day Adventist Church. The congregation had decided they didn't want a metal building as their place of worship, so they listed it for sale at $5,000 with the condition that the buyer would have to take it down and move it to his or her own property.

I thought it was a pretty good deal, a cheap way to get a new building. So Curtis, Joyce, and I and the kids went to disassemble it—me and Curtis doing the heavy work while Joyce and the kids took the hundreds of screws and washers that came from the building (worth five cents apiece) and put them into buckets so we could reconstruct it in the wrecking yard. The building did not turn out to be as good of a deal as I had hoped, however. I found out to pour a new cement slab the size we needed for a proper floor would run about $10,000. Good buy or not, we did it, and now we had a real store that we could add onto and grow.

About the same time as I was working on the building, my older brother, Ray, who was only thirty-seven, was dying from cancer. It came on fast, and all of us took shifts at the hospital to be with him. I'd work at the yard all day and then spend half the night with Ray at his bedside. Like the war, it was another example to me of how fragile life could be and how you needed to make every minute count. As I saw the effects Ray's death had on his surviving wife and kids, it also made me think even harder about the real reason I wanted to be successful—so I could take care of my family.

Stand Out from the Crowd

Even with the larger building to display parts, I knew that to really compete with other auto dismantlers in the Sacramento region, I would need to do something different. I just couldn't realistically keep every make and model part stocked like the larger dismantlers with more money and space. But I knew of some dismantlers like Al Parker in Citrus Heights who was doing well specializing in only Rambler parts at a small two-acre yard. All the larger dismantlers sold their Rambler parts to him and sent Rambler customers his way because they preferred stocking only hot-selling items that had a high demand. Because Al was the only specialized Rambler dealer in the area, he could draw customers from a large geographical area.

I took a trip to LA to meet with the king of specialization—Marv Schmidt, who owned a Chevrolet-only yard that served the entire LA Basin and was extremely successful. Marv's yard consisted of a large building to display parts and a small area across the street, about an eighth of an acre, that he dismantled the cars in. It was an extremely efficient operation. Marv and I eventually became good friends, and Marv became a mentor for me.

I decided that if Al Parker could make a good business selling Rambler parts, and Marv could be so successful specializing in Chevrolet, that was what I wanted to do.

I continued my research by flying to Seattle and meeting with Don Fitz of Fitz Auto Wreckers, who had several different types of specialty yards, including a General Motors yard, a Ford yard, a Chrysler Yard, a foreign car yard, and a Pinto/Vega yard. Seeing his success added more fuel to my enthusiasm to specialize.

I came back and told Curtis that if we were going to compete, we needed to specialize in a car the other dismantlers in town didn't want to carry. At the time Chrysler, Dodge, and Plymouth were not cars dismantlers wanted to have because they weren't hot-selling items. So we made a decision to specialize in Chrysler, Dodge, and Plymouth.

All the other dismantlers thought I was crazy. But they were more than willing to sell us their Chrysler parts that weren't moving and send business our way so they could continue to stock more-popular items.

My friend and brother-in-law Mike James says I'm not afraid to break the mold and go where no one else has gone before. I guess I just don't like people telling me I can't do something. When people tell me, "Willis, you can't do that," it just pushes me to show them I can. It wasn't that I thought I was better than anybody; I just always thought if you wanted something bad enough and worked hard enough for it, it would happen.

And it did. Soon I was drawing on a large area of customers who needed Chrysler parts because other dismantlers didn't have them. In any one area, there wasn't a big demand for Chrysler parts, which is why most dismantlers didn't want to carry them. But in the entire area including Sacramento, Stockton, Marysville, and Yuba City, there was a big demand. There were pockets of General Motors and Ford specialty yards but not Chrysler, so we were filling a need for a big area.

It was also cheaper to stock Chrysler parts. At the time we were still partly in the scrap business, so we could buy all the junk Chrysler cars for thirty-five to forty dollars whereas we were paying seventy-five to one hundred dollars for General Motors junk cars. I could go to an auction and buy a wrecked Dodge Polara for twenty-five cents on a dollar compared to a Chevrolet. So I could buy parts cheaper, but the parts were just as valuable, especially since no one else carried them.

Before we specialized, Curtis and I were running between $3,500 and $5,000 worth of parts a month at Mather. After specializing, we were running around $3,500 worth of parts a day.

Sometimes You Have to Take Big Risks to Get Big Rewards

With all the extra demand, I needed more money to buy more cars and continue to grow the business.

I again turned to the paper and read about Small Business Administration (SBA) loans. I signed over everything I had as collateral against a $50,000 loan, which was a tremendous amount of money at the time.

I didn't mind doing that because I knew I was going to make money. Again, failure wasn't even something that crossed my mind. One of the conditions of the loan was that all the money had to be spent on inventory, so I started going out and buying all the cars I could at car auctions.

One of my regular stops was Bob's Tow Service (BTS) in Vallejo—an insurance auto auction that sold whole cars for the insurance industry. If people are in a car accident and their vehicle is totaled, the insurance company pays out the claim and then brings the car to a place like BTS to recover some of the cost. BTS auctions the car off to auto dismantlers or rebuilders, who may use it for its parts or to repair.

Before I had the loan, I used to spend between $2,000 and $3,000 a week on wrecked cars at BTS. But with the SBA loan, I could now spend $10,000 a week on cars. And as fast as I could bring in the inventory, Curtis was selling it. We were sittin' in some high cotton.

As a result, we asked for and received an extension on the loan so we could continue to buy cars. It was a turning point for the business, as it was the first time we could really grow. But with all the inventory going in and out, we needed a more efficient way to track it.

Technology Is Your Friend

At the time, most people kept paper records of all their parts. But I was one of the first in the business to computerize inventory—an idea I got from my buddy Marv Schmidt.

I spent $110,000 on a large reel-to-reel computer—about double the amount most people spent on a house at the time. The reels themselves were fourteen inches in diameter and stored all the information about the business and its inventory. Every night, new reels were put on the computer to back up the information. This resulted in boxes and boxes of reels. Today, an iPhone could probably hold the same amount of data.

Curtis remembers that other people thought I was crazy (or stupid—or maybe both) to spend so much money on a computer for a wrecking yard. But I was never afraid to spend money on technology if it could help us be more efficient. And it turned out that the whole industry would end up computerizing once they saw the benefits it gave people like me and Marv.

As large and foreign as this machine seemed back then, it paid off because it gave me a complete picture of the business and the inventory, which in turn gave me more knowledge and control over the yard, which helped me make more money.

For example, the computerized system could tell me in a few keystrokes not just how many of each type of make and model doors were in the yard but could also tell me how many right doors we had, how many left doors we had, and what color they all were. If we had a lot of side doors that were the same color, I would discount them to move the inventory. But if we had only one right green Volare door, for example, I could charge customers more because it was harder to find and I could justify the price, which they usually paid because it saved them time and money from having to paint it. This allowed us to move parts faster and maximize our profits.

The computer also kept track of the hot-selling items. For example, after we computerized we learned that we sold a lot of right front fenders and left front doors—although I don't know why. So I made sure we had those in stock. I also started dismantling the right front doors—which didn't sell as frequently. That way, if a customer needed door glass or a door motor, which didn't have to come from a specific side, I could sell them out of the doors that weren't selling very often. This allowed us to still move these parts but not take away from other sales. The customers were happy because they didn't have to pay for a whole door, and we were getting money for inventory that might have otherwise just sat there.

I did other things that other dismantlers looked at me funny for too, although not for long. For example, all the wrecking yards around Sacramento had agreed to use the same size ad—a little tiny ad—in the yellow pages because it was really inexpensive. Well that didn't make any sense to me, so I went and bought a half-page, color ad. Curtis jokes that all the other dismantlers were mad at me for a while because they had to do the same thing to compete. I went big—they went big. I wanted to take it to the next level, and the rest of the guys had to try to keep up.

Learn from Others

Now that I had this computer that told me exactly what parts I needed and what would sell, I used that info when my buddy David March, who had a specialized Ford-dismantling yard, and I went on our yearly buying spree up and down the West Coast.

We'd go in to a yard and notice they had four of the same engines for $500 each and pick them all up for $250 each. They were moving their inventory and getting money for parts that weren't selling, and we were getting a deal.

I'd also use the trip to mine other wrecking yards for ideas I could take home and implement at Mather. We'd suck in all their ideas, and they didn't care if they told us because we weren't direct competitors. So I would learn a lot about what they did that worked and what didn't work, like how they were handling antifreeze and tires as environmental regulations weren't yet developed. Their experiences helped make our company better.

Although the company was booming, and Curtis and I were working very well together, Curtis was at a point in his life when he didn't want to work so hard. He had a new wife and wanted to spend more time with her. He pitched an idea to me that he would work at the yard for six months a year and then I could work the other six months so we both could have half a year off.

But I knew this was an exciting time for Mather. I had an idea to buy OEM (original equipment manufacturer) parts from Chrysler and had also thought about going to Taiwan to buy aftermarket sheet metal. I was also thinking about opening up a second specialty yard. But I couldn't do all I wanted to do by only working part-time.

So I offered to buy out Curtis. We each went home that night and wrote down a number—me, how much I was willing to pay, and

Curtis, how much he was willing to take for his half of the business. The next day we showed each other the numbers and worked out a deal. Turns out our numbers were very close, and we reached an agreement almost right away.

Find Ways to Open Doors

About that time I read in a magazine that Lee Iacocca had taken over Chrysler. Iacocca was the former president of Ford. He was known for engineering the Mustang. Also the Pinto, but he would probably prefer to be remembered for the Mustang. Mr. Iacocca had come to Chrysler to try to revive it. He had decided to shut down the production of Volares and Aspens as part of the process. Well, I looked at that and realized that if they were shutting down production plants, they were probably going to have a lot of Volare and Aspen parts just sitting around.

Just like my dad might have, I turned to my wife, Joyce, and said, "I'm going to Detroit to see Mr. Iacocca, and I am going to make some money."

I called up a friend of mine, Peter Kay. Peter was a retired bird colonel over at Mather Air Force Base and a big customer of mine. He collected Chrysler Imperials and Corvairs, so he was always looking for parts for his next project. I wanted the company on the trip, and Peter thought it would be fun. Turns out it was a good call. Peter was a useful companion.

Being a colonel, retired or otherwise, meant Peter wasn't deterred very easily. He didn't take no for an answer. When we showed up in Detroit, we found out pretty quick that we couldn't just walk up to Lee Iacocca's office and have a sit-down meeting with him. So Peter did the next best thing. He looked up the head of procurement for Chrysler in the company directory. Then he went and printed up some fake business cards real quick. We went back to the Chrysler lobby and walked right up to the front desk clerk to hand over a card and say that we had an appointment.

Of course, it was a big lie. A convincing one, but a lie. Thankfully, the clerk took one look at Peter and figured he knew what he was doing.

Out came the visitor badges and the directions to the procurement office. After a few minutes, we tracked down the person in charge of shutting down the plants.

Now I'll grant you, they were a little concerned that two random guys from California got past security and into the procurement office. But the man in charge did agree to sit down with us. By the time we were done, I walked out of there with a sales list of all the parts available to bid on from the shutdown plants.

It's Okay to Have Too Much of a Good Thing—If You Get Them Cheap Enough

I didn't meet Lee Iacocca, but I did get my foot in the door to buy OEM Chrysler parts. That magazine article sent me into a new sort of business. But to be honest, I hadn't really put together what I was getting myself into.

I'd been going to auctions my whole life, but this wasn't like any auction I'd ever been to. We weren't bidding on one or two items at a time. These were factory parts, so we were bidding on four hundred bumpers, eight hundred rear ends, and two thousand fenders at a time. You had to buy them in bulk or not at all. It was another league altogether.

So there I was with this big list. I figured I needed to start small. Maybe carburetors. I looked at the list and saw that they had three thousand four-barrel and two thousand two-barrel carburetors listed. Well, at the time a four-barrel was selling for about $275 new and a two-barrel got about $150. The parts from the factory were new. But because they were new, they came in crates made for assembly lines, not consumer packaging. And on top of that, there were an assortment of years, makes, models, and motor sizes.

Well, I knew I couldn't afford to bid very much per unit. I just didn't have that kind of cash. So I bid the four-barrels at $15 each and the two-barrels at $7.50 each. I figured that half the barrels meant half the price. Yeah, it was just dumb now that I think about it. But dumb or not, I won the bid.

Then they showed up back home at the yard. I wasn't really expecting to win, and then there were just all those carburetors. That was a *lot* of carburetors. It was kind of overwhelming. But it was also a big opportunity. So I looked around and figured I could wholesale them to other yards. I'd charge $110 each, and if the wrecker wanted ten at a time, I'd drop the price to $95. That would still earn me an $80 profit. Not bad.

We sorted everything out and started selling. We ended up with about five hundred in the mix, though, that we couldn't identify. The serial numbers didn't match up with anything on the Chrysler inventory list, so we didn't have any idea what motor they would fit. I put them to the side, figuring I'd deal with them later.

The parts were selling pretty well, so I headed back to Detroit to do some more buying. I had a little extra time on that trip, so I decided to take a tour of a motorhome plant Chrysler was closing. Selling all those parts for Chrysler made me one of eight major buyers in the country, so they gave me pretty free rein.

I was walking around that motorhome lot when I came across a wall full of red International motorhome engines. The engines were complete except for one part—the carburetors. I checked the serial numbers for that part and realized I'd solved my little mystery. I was sitting on five hundred International motorhome carburetors. I mentioned my little inventory quirk to the folks at International and headed back to Mather.

It wasn't long before I got a call from the people who had bought all those International engines. Seems they needed carburetors. I sold them five hundred for ninety-five dollars apiece.

Business was booming, and I was sittin' in higher and higher cotton.

After moving through that inventory, I made another trip out to Detroit and decided to give radiators a try. They had these big crates of new radiators designed for Volares, Aspens, and Cordobas. Since I'd been in the scrap business, I knew that each radiator had five dollars' worth of copper in it, so I figured I'd bid seven dollars each on the lot. That way I could sell the radiators, and whatever I couldn't move would still get me five dollars off the copper.

A little while later, a truck showed up at the yard with five hundred radiators. We lined everything out and started to sell them. About two weeks later, though, another truck showed up—full of radiators. Now, that was a lot of radiators, and I hadn't bought them.

I got on the phone with Chrysler and got the story.

Turns out my connections at Chrysler just figured I'd want these too, so they just shipped them straight to me, no questions asked.

That was a nice sentiment, but I didn't have the money to pay for *another* five hundred radiators. It was too much for me to pay up front, so Chrysler and I came to a deal to pay for them over ninety days.

Two weeks later, another truck full of radiators showed up unordered.

They offered me six months on that load. I was becoming Chrysler's favorite way of getting rid of parts, and I didn't mind.

Find Creative Solutions

I started selling so many new Chrysler parts that Chrysler itself started to feel some heat. Chrysler dealers were getting upset because if they wanted a four-barrel carburetor for one of their cars, they had to pay $180 to get it discounted from Chrysler. But I was selling the same carburetor on my shelves for $110. Problem was, dealers couldn't buy from me; they had to get certified parts directly from Chrysler.

Chrysler found a unique solution by asking me to take over a marine dealership that was struggling in the area. I don't know anything about boats, and I told them that. But Chrysler told me not to worry about that. All I had to do, they said, was put the parts in his shop, and they'd sell them for me. I figured I had nothing to lose, so I agreed and became an industrial dealer, at least on paper. That allowed me to continue to purchase inexpensive parts and sell them to Chrysler dealers, as well as use the Chrysler name and logo outside my shop. All I had to do was ship out the marine motors whenever Chrysler faxed me an order. I even got a small commission for it. Now that was a good deal.

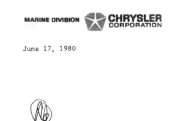

MARINE & INDUSTRIAL SALES OFFICE

MARINE DIVISION CHRYSLER CORPORATION

June 17, 1980

Mr. Willis Johnson
Mather Auto
4095 Happy Lane
Sacramento, CA 95826

Subject: DIESEL DISTRIBUTOR CONTRACT

Dear Willis:

Welcome to the Chrysler team - your fully executed Industrial Diesel Distributor Contract is enclosed.

I feel that we will have many years of successful association.

Your penetration of the diesel market in your area looks encouraging.

Very truly yours,

CHRYSLER CORPORATION
MARINE DIVISION

L. D. CARUFEL
Sales Manager
Industrial Engines

LDC/spy
Encl.
cc: P. Kay
J. Hummon

6501 HARPER AVE. P.O. BOX 2718 DETROIT MICHIGAN 48288

First Impressions Matter

Of course, sometimes you get the best information right in front of you. Sure, you should read the paper and talk to other folks in your business. But keeping your eyes open can make a big difference too.

We were growing so fast that I was running all over California buying cars to keep up with demand. We were pulling a lot of business through Chrysler directly, but we were still buying wrecks all over the state and dismantling them for the parts we weren't getting directly. I was flying to LA to buy some more cars pretty regularly, and as I drove up to San Francisco to catch a plane south one day, I noticed all the cabs at the airport. I saw that the Desoto, Luxor, and Yellow cabs were all Volares and Aspens. Well, now, if you are running a fleet that size you're going to need parts to keep it going. And I was the man to talk to about affordable Volare parts. So I tracked down one of the owners of Desoto cabs to have a talk with him.

I sat down and offered to wholesale him parts at fifty cents on the dollar to maintain his fleet of three hundred cabs, as long as he ordered $500 worth of parts at a time. Being as he didn't know me, though, he decided to test the waters with a small order at first. Fair enough, I thought. He ordered about ten front rotors, some upper control arms, suspensions, and rear ends. Even though it wasn't as big an order as I wanted, it was just big enough.

I filled the order myself and delivered it. The owner, impressed that I'd taken care of it so quickly, made a bigger order right away—one hundred front rotors, twenty left and right control arms, some upper control arms, twenty rear ends, and seven transmissions. It was the big order I was hoping for. I knew right away that this could lead to something even better. With any deal, you want to treat folks right, like you'd like to be treated. And first impressions matter.

I went back to my yard and loaded up my transporter and my delivery truck. I hooked the truck onto the back and towed it all the way back to San Francisco. When I pulled into Desoto, I saw the owner laughing and joking with two other guys I didn't know. I had a bad feeling about that. I was worried they weren't going to take all the parts after all. It looked like the deal might have gone sour and I'd made the trip for nothing.

I climbed out of the truck and stepped up to the men on the lot. The owner turned to me and said, "Willis, I want you to meet the owner of the Yellow Cab Company and the owner of Luxor Cabs. Yellow has six hundred cabs, and Luxor has four hundred. They want parts too."

I couldn't believe it. I was sittin' in high cotton yet again.

Do Your Research

I was doing so much business with the cab companies, I started to print up catalogues for them, and they started ordering so much I was afraid I'd run out of parts.

I called my buddy Don Fitz with the Chrysler yard in Seattle, as well as Danny's Auto Salvage in Tulsa, Oklahoma, which also specialized in Chrysler parts. I started buying parts from them to supplement my own inventory. I didn't mind helping them out because they weren't my direct competitors, and it also helped me succeed.

Then there was a bad train wreck outside of Roseville in the Sierras. The train was carrying new Chrysler LeBarons and some Cadillacs and General Motors cars too and had completely derailed on its side in two-foot-high snow, damaging all the cars.

I found out the wrecked cars had been taken to the Roseville train yard and went over to look at them. While General Motors wanted all their cars crushed, Chrysler decided to auction off all their cars because the company needed the money. I bought them all, about fifty, and sold all the brand-new motors and transmissions to the cab companies. My worry about keeping up with the demand for parts was put to rest, at least partially.

I still never seemed to be able to find enough fenders, hoods, grills, and bumpers. Once again, I got an idea from a newspaper after reading about new sheet metal being shipped in from Taiwan. It is kind of ironic that my dad, who didn't know how to read, taught me to get ideas from newspapers and magazines. But it was a great lesson.

He taught me that you have to do your research and that if you don't stay on top of reading about other people's ideas, you never come up with ideas yourself. It's good to learn from others.

So after reading about the metal from Taiwan, I did more research and found out the metal was exactly like the metal you could purchase in the United States except for one thing. The holes were drilled a little differently so it had to be altered slightly to fit right. I thought I could still sell them to the public if I told them how to work around this—show them how to fix it. But the body shops and insurance companies weren't interested in the Taiwan metal because they weren't allowed to use parts that weren't factory approved.

So I did more research. I found out a Volare fender that I could sell for $180 would only cost me $15 in Taiwan. That was a profit margin I couldn't ignore, so I flew to Taiwan, taking Peter Kay along again for the ride. We met with a shipping company called Eastern Dragon, who explained that we would have to buy a whole container load in order to ship it back to the United States The containers were huge, so I filled it with five hundred right fenders, five hundred left fenders, and hoods and grills. The container took six weeks to arrive from order to delivery because of loading, shipping, and then trucking it to our facility, but I had to pay for it before it left the dock. That meant having to wait for a return on my investment. I learned to time it so I would have two or three containers on the water at any time, so they would hit the States every two weeks. I'd then sell those parts to the cab companies and over the counter. It proved to be a gold mine. Once again, I was sittin' in high cotton.

Don't Get Lazy

Don't get me wrong, though. I had my not-so-great moments too. We all do. There especially were times when I thought I was buying too much.

For example, I saw a bid sheet for iron and noniron items that were coming from Chrysler's Direct Connection Division, which was their hot rod and muscle car division. I figured anything coming from direct connection had to be good, so I bid on it without really knowing what it was.

Basically, I got lazy.

I ended up getting the whole truck load for about $2,500. When the truck pulled in late one afternoon, all the guys in the yard were excited to see what was in it, including me.

We opened up the back of the truck, and there were all these pieces of cardboard, probably an inch thick and eight inches wide and two feet long. The truck was stuffed full of these pieces of cardboard, and for a while, none of us could figure out what they were. Then it hit us—these were patterns. Similar to patterns used to cut out cloth for a shirt or a dress, these patterns were used to cut out wood paneling for vans.

I had bought a whole truckload of something that had no value whatsoever. This was my version of the Tampax my father had once bought thinking they were compacts.

Joyce and the crew laughed at me, and I was pretty upset at my mistake. As we pulled the cardboard out of the truck, however, one of the guys made another discovery.

"Hey, Willis, I think I found some good stuff," he told me.

The last six feet of the truck, all the way in the front, was filled with Hemi motors, 340 engines, and other high-performance parts that were valued at about $25,000 to $30,000. Because it had been so heavy, they had put it in the front and packed the cardboard around it.

My Tampax turned into compacts after all. It was a fun deal, but it did teach me something: stop buying things without seeing them! They started calling me Lucky Dog after that. I was lucky I didn't get burned after doing something so foolish as buying something I knew nothing about.

My brother-in-law, Mike James, was a little kinder about it. He thinks it wasn't just luck but the way I constantly think about and plan things—seeing opportunities others don't.

"You may not be highly educated and may not always use the proper words at the proper time, but you know what you want, and you push until you're successful," he said.

But I knew that truck could have easily turned out a bust too. Luck was on my side. And God. He always had my back, it seems.

Don't Rest on Your Laurels

God just always seemed to point me in the right direction. Such was the case on another trip I took to Taiwan. While there, I visited a company called Modine Radiator, where they manufactured brand-new radiators at a fraction of the cost. When I returned from Taiwan, I decided to open my own radiator company and called it Today Radiator, stocking it with the radiators from Taiwan I purchased for fifteen cents on the dollar for what you had to pay for them in America. Today Radiator was separate from Mather and did business from a storefront in a strip mall, selling to the public and to body shops. I let people exchange their old radiators for a discount on the new ones and then rebuilt the old radiators to sell at Mather.

The Mather yard continued to succeed. But I was concerned. While Chrysler was a cash cow for now, as Detroit continued to stop making cars and shutting down plants, it would be harder to do business because fewer people would have Chrysler vehicles to repair. I needed another way of making money in case Chrysler dried up. This was no time to rest on my laurels.

As I attended auto auctions, I noticed there were more mini-trucks than ever before. The 1973 oil crisis had sparked the popularity of more fuel-efficient vehicles like the Chevy Luv, Ford Courier, and Datsun pickups. Yet there were no yards that specialized in these unique vehicles.

Seeing another opportunity, I opened Mather Mini-Truck in West Sacramento. A friend of mine who wanted to retire had a forklift dealership on about two acres and leased it to me. Using the model that worked for me in the past, I chose to predismantle the trucks and rack the parts. I shipped in aftermarket sheet metal from Taiwan to fill the inventory and told other dismantlers I was specializing so they could send mini-truck business my way.

It was another instant hit. As the business grew, Datsun turned into Nissan, the Ford Courier turned into the Ford Ranger, and the Chevy Luv went to the S10. But the success of the business remained constant.

Meanwhile, Curtis had decided retirement wasn't a viable option after all, and he needed to make a living again. He opened his own wrecking yard in Woodland, and we continued to help each other out. We also enjoyed a friendly rivalry as we often bid against each other on cars at Bob's Tow Service (BTS). At that time, bids were put in envelopes and then counted at the end of the day, much like a silent auction.

There was a percentage of cars no one wanted because they were nothing but metal. Curtis would go into BTS and bid $49.95 on one of these cars, and then I'd go in, not knowing what he bid, and bid $51.95. Curtis and I had played Monopoly and Risk all our lives, so this was just another nonverbal game we tried to beat each other at to see who would get the car.

I was also friends with the owner of BTS, Bob Kukuruza. Bob playfully called Joyce and me the Dodge Boys, and I would bring Bob donuts and visit with him during auctions. Bob had been semiretired for a while, letting his sons run the auction while he ran the tow part of the business. We also shared the same accountant—Bob Stewart.

Bob Kukuruza's sons had decided they no longer wanted the business, and Bob considered selling it. One day, while talking to Bob Stewart, Bob expressed that he wished he knew someone who might want to buy it. Bob Stewart told him he thought I would and then called me to tell me about the opportunity.

Bob wanted $1 million for the business—an astronomical number. The trucks and tractors that came with the business were only valued at about $100,000, and the deal did not include the land. BTS was bringing in only $65,000 pretax annually selling cars for insurance companies like the California State Automobile Association (AAA).

But I knew what I could do with that company, how far I could take it. Expanding my business ventures with an auto auction would help me diversify but also made good sense as the businesses were compatible. Bob and his sons had mainly set the business on cruise control over the last several years, and I felt that with some focus, the potential for growth was huge.

There was only one thing that bothered me. AAA was Bob's biggest seller, and I was one of the biggest buyers. I didn't want to buy BTS and either lose my biggest source of cars—or worse, be the reason BTS lost its biggest customer. I asked Bob to talk to AAA and make sure they were okay with me taking over the business. They agreed to the deal as long as I didn't have access to the sealed bids. The sealed bids would stay locked up, with only AAA having the key so the bidding system would remain fair.

I agreed to buy BTS, but I couldn't swing a deal of that magnitude by myself. So I called my friend Peter Kay—the same one who helped me get into see the procurement director at Chrysler and who went with me to Taiwan. Peter had expressed to me more than once he would like to go into business with me, and this seemed like the perfect opportunity. We each put up $50,000 as a down payment for the yard. But Bob wanted me to use Mather as collateral for the rest of the money. We could pay the rest in payments over time, with an option to purchase the land.

I told Peter that if I had to take the risk of putting Mather up as collateral, I wanted controlling interest. Peter agreed, and in November of 1982, I became 51 percent owner of BTS, while Peter became a 49 percent owner.

My sister Bonnie said she will never forget how excited Peter and I were. We were excited to buy a salvage auction and to be branching out from the wrecking business. It was a big step, one that would change my life forever.

Find Good Partners

At about the same time I was working out a deal to buy BTS, a friend of mine who owned a wrecking yard in Grass Valley went with me and Joyce to Los Angeles to attend a trade show, along with his wife. While there, we heard from some other attendees about a new way of wrecking cars.

They told me there was a whole new concept that had been started in LA and that was really successful; it was called Pick-A-Part. As I learned more, I decided to skip the convention and go look at this new kind of wrecking yard instead, so all four of us drove up to Pick-A-Part, still wearing our convention clothes.

The first thing I noticed was that the parking lot was huge—about three acres. No wrecking yard has that much of a parking lot because no wrecking yard has that many customers. But this one was full. People were lined up, and they were paying fifty cents at the door just to get in—not even to buy anything.

I thought to myself, *I don't know what they are selling back there, but I want in on the action!*

We all got in line, but they wouldn't let our wives in with open toed-shoes. We loaned them our spare shoes from our suitcases, and we all went in wearing men's shoes.

Inside, all the cars were lined up on stands after being depolluted. Customers would find the car they wanted, take off the part they needed themselves, and bring it up to a trailer with bulletproof windows where people lined up to pay. No one helped them, except to take their money, making the overhead minimal. And there were at least eight hundred customers at the yard doing business.

I thought, *This is cool! I'm going to do this!*

The convention long forgotten, Joyce and I returned to Northern California, and I started to look for a suitable location for my own self-service parts business. I found 3A Auto Dismantling in South Sacramento whose owner, Bill Aston, wanted to retire. I made him what was becoming my standard deal—$100,000 down with payments and interest. They would lease the land with an option to buy it in ten years.

The problem was, though, I really didn't have the money to do BTS and the self-service yard at the same time. I knew I was going to run out of money if I didn't watch what I did. But I wanted to do both. I needed to figure out how.

I had worked with a company called Horizon Advertising in Sacramento on radio and television ads for my other stores and had become good friends with the owners, Dick Nelson and Doug Behrle. They, too, had told me they were interested in going into business with me. I guess they knew I knew how to make money. So I asked if they wanted to be partners in the self-service dismantling business I was starting. They agreed, along with another retired colonel I knew, Mr. Patton. Joe Fazo also said he'd go in. Combined, the partners owned 49 percent, and I owned 51 percent.

After buying 3A Auto Dismantling, we went to work to try to clean it up for the new business. It was a true junkyard, a real mess. Joe and I had to spend a long time cleaning it up, including auctioning what we could and crushing what we couldn't. We also had to level the yard and create an area to pay. It took a couple of months to get everything done and get about five hundred cars up on stands.

While all the work was happening, we were trying to figure out what to call this new venture. We couldn't call it Pick-A-Part like the one in LA. We finally thought of the name U-Pull-It, and Dick and Doug got busy on a marketing plan. They painted everything a bright orange color to get people's attention and made U-Pull-It T-shirts to give away to customers during the grand opening. Horizon also bought radio and newspaper ads announcing there was a new way to buy parts.

The day U-Pull-It opened, more than eight hundred people came and paid their fifty cents to get in. All that hard work and advertising had paid off, and we had another successful business on our hands. It was unbelievable how fast it took off.

Learn from Wal-Mart

What made the U-Pull-It model unique was the high volume of cars it could turn around. I liken it to the Wal-Mart of dismantling. But it was also a little like the old days of Mather because there was a lot of scrap iron. To keep everything cheap and to be able to retain a high volume, U-Pull-It dealt mostly in end-of-life cars. It got its cars by running ads in the paper announcing, "We'll buy your junk car." How much we paid for that car depended on how far we had to tow it and how popular the parts on that make and model were.

Popular makes and models would sit out for about thirty days while people pulled what they wanted from it. Less-popular cars would sit for sixty days. At the end of the allotted time, what was left was crushed, and fresh cars brought in with fresh parts.

At $70 a ton you can get about $140 for a two-ton car. But if you can sell another $100 or $200 worth of parts out of it, you are doubling your money. Then you multiply that by one hundred cars a day, and that's where the money comes in because it's not about how good the parts are on it. If you have three hundred car doors that you would normally crush and you can sell some of them for $5 or $6 each, you're that much further ahead.

We could do this because the customers at a self-service yard like U-Pull-It were also different than customers at my other businesses. These were people who didn't have a lot of money and were barely getting by. They needed to get their cars running as cheaply as possible to get to work the next day and oftentimes were fixing it themselves. By contrast, Mather dealt mostly with body shops and mechanics, people wanting late-model parts that were guaranteed and as perfect as possible.

Most of the customers at U-Pull-It were driving cars just like the ones inside the gates. In some cases, customers would even sell their cars in exchange for one that was slightly better inside. They could buy a car there for $300, drive it until it barely worked, and bring it back a few months later and sell it for $50. Then they could buy another $300 one again. It was a cheap way to maintain transportation.

U-Pull-It was also a popular stop for buyers from Mexico, who came with semitrucks and filled them with fenders, radiators, and other parts they would then take over the border and resell. We would give them a discount for buying more than $5,000 worth of parts.

The model for U-Pull-It was simple. It didn't matter what the condition of a part was; all parts of the same kind cost the same amount of money. That put the liability on the person buying it, not the person selling. It benefitted the customers to hunt for the best part they could because they were paying the same amount.

In the end, U-Pull-It also had three revenue streams—the gate fee, the parts sales, and scrap iron. That was just three more reasons to like the business, as far as I was concerned.

It also had another by-product of business. Because many of the cars were abandoned or forgotten, much of what was left inside had also been forgotten. We created a thrift store out of these items—baby strollers, CD cases, clothing, and more. Our customers, always looking for a deal, loved the bargains, and it provided yet one more revenue stream to the mix.

Seize Opportunities

There was opportunity everywhere, and I seized it. When I purchased 3A Auto Dismantling for U-Pull-It, the business had also come with a parts house and a radiator repair shop. I kept the parts house and called it Mather Auto Parts so people who purchased parts at U-Pull-It could go next door and buy the gaskets and other items they needed to put it together. I then moved the newly purchased radiator shop to become part of the booming Today Radiator business.

I was sittin' in high cotton, running on all cylinders with the Mather Chrysler yard, the mini-truck yard, Today Radiator, Mather Auto Parts, and U-Pull-It. I had also decided to specialize yet again, opening up a foreign auto parts yard next to U-Pull-It under the now well-known Mather name. Foreign cars had become more popular, and I could ship in foreign parts from Taiwan for pennies on the dollar for Datsuns, Toyotas, and Fords. I also sold aftermarket sheet metal from the foreign parts yard.

But I still wanted to increase business, especially at the specialized yards. I started a dismantling magazine so I could advertise and allowed all specialized yards in the Sacramento area to purchase full-page ads in it, which I then direct mailed to body shops, mechanics, and insurance companies. I didn't start the magazine to make money but to be a tool that I, along with other specialized dismantlers, could use to get more business.

At first, we just called the magazine *Specialized Magazine*, a boring name I didn't care for. We needed to think of something better. Then I remembered from my days growing up on a farm how farmers would store their grain together in a co-op and how other businesses would form similar alliances for a mutual benefit. Since the magazine was a co-op of parts dealers using it for the mutual benefit of advertising, I decided to call it *Copart* instead.

A short time later, I also incorporated the magazine as a C corporation to protect myself against any claims against the magazine and allow it to be taxed separately from me as its own entity. But then the recession hit in the mid-1970s and gas prices began to soar. Other specialized dealers started cutting their spending and stopped advertising, so *Copart* sat idle.

I had my hands in a lot of stuff, so I relied on good managers at all my businesses to keep them all going. I had Joe manage the day-to-day business at U-Pull-It, while Peter Kay ran BTS. I was advised by my accountant to think of incorporating BTS too—to protect both me and Peter from any liability and keep taxes separate. I had already paid $600 to incorporate the name Copart, and I wasn't using it. To save another $600, I decided to just move the C-Corp over and change the name of BTS to Copart.

Solve Your Own Problems

Copart and U-Pull-It continued to grow almost simultaneously. Joe Fazo and I decided to build on the momentum, and along with our other U-Pull-It partners, we opened a second U-Pull-It location in Fairfield, California, which is between Sacramento and the Bay Area. Joe did most of the legwork to make sure it was set up like the first U-Pull-It. The goal was to create a cookie-cutter operation in which each U-Pull-It location had the same look, feel, and business model, thereby creating a strong brand.

It was evident to me that U-Pull-It was becoming the cash cow, replacing the Mather Chrysler yard as the most successful of my business ventures. We were turning so many cars at the first U-Pull-It location that the DMV couldn't keep up with us.

When each car was purchased and the title changed, we had to have the people in my office fill out the paperwork for the DMV by hand. The paperwork came in big printed books that the DMV mailed out, with each book handling about twenty-five car transactions that were three pages each. U-Pull-It was turning about one hundred cars per day—or four books' worth. We had to order these books by the pallet to keep up, and I couldn't help but think how much money the state was paying to print all these books out. Sometimes I couldn't get enough books sent to us in time to keep up with the business. It was putting us in a real bind because by law you had to fill out the paperwork on these cars within twenty-four hours. It was just all this paper, and we had to wait to get these books, and it was slowing us down.

Instead of waiting for the DMV to find a better way, I went to them and proposed a solution. I would develop a way to create electronic forms and print them from a computer, thereby eliminating the need for the DMV to send out the books at all, saving them money and my business valuable time.

I spent about $40,000 building the computerized system for the state of California. Now we could go to the computer and fill out all the paperwork needed and didn't have to wait for books. It sped up the whole process and was an example of how it pays to fix something yourself instead of waiting for someone else to solve the problem for you.

Be in the Right Place at the Right Time

At almost the same time I was expanding and improving U-Pull-It, I also opened up a second Copart yard in Sacramento. Right after that second Copart yard opened, there was a massive flood in Yuba City, and the new Copart yard in Sacramento filled up with the cars with water damage. Whether it was luck, God looking out for me again, or both, I was again at the right place at the right time.

Copart was growing, but U-Pull-It was still the star of the show, and the second U-Pull-It location was doing so well so quickly that Joe and I started talking right away about opening yet a third U-Pull-It yard.

We wanted to open the third location in a low-income area where people needed a place to go to get parts to fix up their own cars. I was especially interested in the Stockton area and thought it would be perfect for the U-Pull-It business model. But Joe wanted a location that was closer to San Francisco, where the cost of living and the cost of opening a yard were much higher.

I deferred to my partner, and we started to look for land in San Francisco. But two weeks later, Joe told me he wanted to end our partnership. He just wanted to do his own thing. He wasn't upset or anything. He just said he did not want to be partners anymore. I understood that, but I was also not in a position after opening these new yards to pay him out. We were on a roll, and I didn't want to lose momentum.

I told him if he didn't want to be partners, that was OK. But I couldn't give him any money. He'd just have to leave and keep his shares of the business. When we sold the company, he could get his money then. Or if I was in a position to buy him out later, that could happen too. But if he wanted out, he would be walking out with shares, not cash.

Joe was fine with that arrangement. He knew I would continue to build up the business, which in turn would make his 27 percent of the business more valuable. But he really wanted to go out on his own. He had sold his own wrecking yard in Grass Valley and had money to invest in something else.

Thirty days later, Joe opened up a self-service yard in Stockton and called it Pick N Pull.

It didn't really bother me because there was a lot of money to go around. I knew Joe wanted to be his own boss in his own yard, and I understood that. So when he did that, I decided to go into Richmond, California, which is a low-income city east of San Francisco. It cost a lot of money because it was in the Bay Area, but I figured it was far enough away from Joe and the other locations that I could carve out a good business that would offset the cost.

Value People's Trust

Prior to opening the Richmond U-Pull-It, AAA Insurance—Copart's largest customer—decided they wanted to open up a training facility in Hayward, also in the East Bay, where they would also store and auction cars. Because of my relationship with them, they turned to me for help. They asked me to design the salvage pool and run it so they could concentrate on the school. I would get the profits from the yard, which would only auction AAA vehicles. In exchange, I waived any storage fees for AAA at my other two Copart yards in Vallejo and Sacramento. The new Hayward yard also saved AAA the cost of towing vehicles from the Bay Area to Vallejo or Sacramento.

It was fair to them and fair to me, so I agreed. They saved a lot of money in towing and storage, and I got to expand the Copart brand with no overhead.

The deal also showed the trust that had built up between me and the insurance company.

Breaking Up Is Hard to Do—but You Still Have to Do It

Peter had been running Copart successfully for a couple of years but had started to lose interest. He was now in his late sixties and wanted to retire. He also owned several race horses and was spending more and more time at the track. Then I got a call from AAA, who told me they hadn't been paid for the cars I had purchased over the past three weeks. I had written checks from Mather and U-Pull-It to Copart for the cars, and the office secretary in Vallejo had been responsible for making sure those payments were made to AAA, so I couldn't figure out what had happened. I drove to the Vallejo yard and confronted Peter.

Peter insisted that the payments had been made and then told me he was going to the track. Well that irritated me, because Peter should be taking the situation more seriously and looking into it. So I stayed behind and started going through the office secretary's desk, where I found my checks in a pile stapled to invoices that had never been processed.

The next day I told Peter that if he was going to run the company, he had to do it right and couldn't do it from the racetrack.

"I have too much invested in this business, including my name and reputation," I said. I told Pete to come up with a number for what he thought his portion of the business was worth, and I would come up with a number for what I thought my portion of the business was worth. The next day we would compare the numbers, and Peter would have a choice; he could either sell to me for his number or buy me out for my number.

"It's up to you," I told him.

When we compared numbers the next day, the difference was about $50,000. But Peter had previously given his sons 9 percent of the business, and his number didn't include their portion. I told Peter it had to be all of the business or nothing. In the end, Peter chose to sell it all to me and pursue his other interests.

Embrace Change

Now full owner of Copart, I started making other changes, including putting up a new building in Vallejo, which had become Copart's headquarters. I also decided to change the auction from sealed bids—in which people wrote down their bid on a piece of paper—to live auctions, where people verbally bid in front of an auctioneer. At the time, live auctions were the new trend in the industry, and I had seen firsthand how they were generating more excitement for the cars and more vigorous bidding. When buyers could hear other buyers bidding on the car, they were also more likely to bid higher. In sealed-bid auctions, they were shooting in the dark because they didn't know what other people were bidding and therefore were not as aggressive.

I also made one more dramatic change. One day during a big auction, I noticed there were about twenty-five people in the parking lot who wanted to come in but couldn't because they weren't licensed dismantlers—a legal rule for bidding on salvage pool cars. Instead, they had asked licensed dismantlers to look at and bid on cars for them.

I had an idea. I called U-Pull-It so they could fax me a sign-in sheet used to sign over customers' liability. I then scratched out the name "U-Pull-It" and wrote "Copart" at the top. Then I told the crowd that if they got permission from a licensed dismantler, they could come in if they signed away their liability. This satisfied the legal requirement. Each guest had to have the buyer number of a licensed dismantler before being granted access, and the buyer was responsible for them.

The result was that the amateur buyers urged the bids up and created more competition, which in turn meant bigger returns.

My longtime friend Jimmy Meeks heard what I was doing and was getting pressure to do the same at his dad's yard. Jimmy's dad had owned a wrecking yard in the South Bay and had decided to specialize in Chrysler, Dodge, and Plymouth after hearing about my success. They had also followed in my footsteps by starting South Bay Salvage, an auto auction. Later Jimmy converted the specialized yard into a self-service yard and used the U-Pull-It name, giving me the gate fees in exchange for being able to use the U-Pull-It brand. I had no other ties to that facility, however.

Jimmy's dad was upset about the deal, thinking paying me all the money from the gate was too much. But the U-Pull-It name drew eight hundred people in a day, making the business a great success, which softened him over time. Jimmy and I were also far enough away we weren't direct competitors, and we often shared ideas.

Make Your Business like Disneyland

I got the inspiration to create new services within my companies from Disneyland.

When I was younger and I went to Disneyland for the first time, Disneyland wasn't just a theme park to me or a place to have fun. Disneyland to me was a model of how to build businesses within a business. I paid a fee just to get in the gate. And then when I went to a restaurant, I paid to eat and drink. Then I paid money at the gift shops. I paid for tickets to the rides. Everything I did was another business. I thought, *Okay, I've got to find a business that has multiple revenue streams within it.* Disneyland taught me about building other revenue streams.

Every time you can add a revenue stream to the same pipeline, the profit margins change drastically. You are putting more through that pipe. That's what I always tried to do in my businesses, and it is how we were successful.

Teach Your Children through the Business

U-Pull-It grew up as my children also grew up. As each of them turned sixteen, I would find them a wrecked vehicle from one of the wrecking yards for them to fix up themselves and drive. The kids had to put up half the money—which Joyce and I would match.

Reba's car was a Plymouth Arrow, a recovered theft that I helped her fix up by finding replacement parts that had been stripped off. Jason got a wrecked Chevy Luv pickup. Inheriting my dad's and my love of cars, Jason took it all apart and put it back together, adding a stereo and other custom features. Tammi wanted a Camaro, so I found her a four-cylinder that had suffered from an interior fire. At the time, I was doing a deal with a friend in Portland who owned a salvage yard. I had him ship everything from the inside of a late-model Camaro he had at his yard down to California for Tammi as part of the deal. It took days for Tammi to clean the inside of the burned car, ripping out burned carpeting and parts until she herself was black from the soot. Then Jason helped her install the clean parts from Oregon.

Joyce and I were sittin' in high cotton from all my business ventures and hard work. We were driving nice cars, had a house with a pool, and could have afforded to buy all the kids new cars. But we had both also known hard times. We wanted our kids to learn how to make money and save money so they would understand the value of a dollar and respect what went into having a car. But I also wanted them to learn a little bit about the business I was in—the business that had supported the family all these years and that was doing so well.

Family Always Comes First

The joy of my success was darkened by the growing ill health of my dad, however. Now living in Yuba City, Dad had previously had a heart attack that inspired him to slow down his drinking and begin to enjoy life more. He had sold all his companies off and had made peace with all of us kids, who had also learned a lot over the years. Dad enjoyed going on trips with Mom, and they would take their fifth wheel to Nevada in the winter where it was warmer. His joints had started to hurt, and the dry, warm air in Nevada suited him better. But on one such trip, the pain got to be so great he had to call me to come and drive them home to Yuba City. I flew there immediately and brought them back to California.

The doctors there at first diagnosed him with lupus, but their treatments weren't working. Dad was starting to lose his motor functions and could no longer do some simple tasks—like scratch an itch.

I would drive to Yuba City two or three nights a week after work to be with Dad—the man I had looked up to all my life and who I shared so many traits with. Finally, I convinced him to come to Sacramento to get a second opinion. The doctors in Sacramento rediagnosed Dad with Lou Gehrig's disease, a progressive and fatal disorder that causes its victims to lose the ability to initiate and control all voluntary movement, although their minds remain strong.

Dad and Mom made the move from Yuba City back to Sacramento, where all of us kids could be closer to them and help as the disease progressed. About one year later, Dad died one morning in his sleep. He was only sixty-five.

Dad was a self-made man and was always larger than life to me. It was really tough losing him. The only problems we ever had happened when he was drinking—but he was always an honest man, a hardworking man, and from my perspective, he knew how to do everything.

I took solace after his death in caring for my mom. I was always a mamma's boy. So we started to take her on vacations with us, and in later years, she moved in with us.

I also took comfort in knowing my dad was proud of what I had accomplished.

I think he always admired what I did. He knew I could handle it and was always a big promoter of me. He did tell me I bought too many carburetors when I went to Chrysler that time. And he did tell me I bought too many cars. He'd always caution that anyone could buy too much of anything. But later when he saw I knew what I was doing, I think he was impressed with what I did.

He was especially impressed that I had purchased BTS. Dad knew Bob Kukuruza and always said the best thing I ever did was to buy BTS and get into auto auctions. He told me it would take me a long way.

Although my dad loved auctions and used them his whole life to sell off his businesses and buy new ones, I'm not sure why he never had an auction of his own. Being good with numbers, I don't know why he didn't become an auctioneer and do it himself. Maybe it was because when you set up an auction, you have to write everything down and then read it off while you are auctioning it. Again, it was probably the fact he couldn't read or write that held him back. I'm sure that was frustrating for him. But I'm grateful my dad passed that love of auctions down to me. I continued to use all my dad taught me to grow the businesses beyond what either of us had ever imagined.

CHAPTER 5

Lessons I Learned as a Teacher

That kid bugs me. He's always asking questions.
—Willis Johnson about Jay Adair,
future CEO of Copart

Give People a Chance

In 1989, a young kid named Jay Adair had just gotten out of high school and to my irritation, started dating my daughter Tammi. When Jay would come over to the house to see Tammi, I would immediately grab a book and head to the bathroom to avoid him. For one, I didn't like the way he looked at my daughter. Then there was just his energy; he couldn't seem to sit still—or be quiet.

But Joyce, as always, saw through my plan and called me out on it.

"Why do you ignore that kid?" she asked me.

"That kid bugs me," I told her. "He's always asking questions. He doesn't know when to stop. I don't want to talk to this kid. I'm tired of talking to him. He wants to know everything!"

Well Joyce kind of set me straight.

"Listen, if our daughter is serious about this boy, which it looks like she is, you can't keep ignoring him," she said. "Just give him a chance."

She was right. And while I wasn't really happy about it, I supposed I better at least try to see what she saw in him. Even if it killed me.

It took a little time, but Ms. Pacman finally broke the ice between Jay and me. We are both extremely competitive, and we would spend hours playing a Ms. Pacman arcade game I had bought for my house. Our wrists would hurt from using the joystick, and our eyes would ache from staring at the screen. But both of us got really good at it—and along the way, we came to like each other.

Jay has a different version of how we got to be friends. He thinks my story about running to the bathroom to avoid him is an exaggeration, and he claims we loved hanging out with each other from the start. He tells me he thought I was cool and full of life. I was just a typical '80s guy with my cowboy boots, Jordache jeans, aviator glasses, and gold chains driving around in a 1984 Corvette and listening to country music. I wasn't trying to be cool. I think Jay was just young and didn't see things straight. Although the Corvette was cool, I admit.

Today most people think of me as the patriarch of Copart—filled with maturity and wisdom. So it is kind of nice that Jay remembers me this way and shares that image of the young gunslinger I once was. Jay said back then I went full-speed into everything—that I was a ball of fire. I guess I was. But while age and wisdom probably have slowed me down a little, I still don't let any moss grow around me. What fun is that?

Back then I would show Jay pictures of Mather, U-Pull-It, and Copart and talk about the businesses. Jay was obviously not just impressed but curious and a little skeptical, I think. He couldn't understand how anyone could make money in junk cars and parts. He grew up in a world where he'd never been to a wrecking yard.

Jay had developed a strong work ethic at a young age thanks to his dad—just like I did from mine. Jay's dad was a chiropractor who also built and owned medical buildings. As early as twelve, Jay would help his dad with construction, learning as he went. To this day people tease Jay because he has absolutely no sports knowledge. He was too busy working to pay attention to sports. While Jay's brother was the captain of the football team, he took a different path. In his family, it was either make money or play ball. He chose to make money. I guess that's another thing we had in common, and it is something I admired about him.

While my world was strange to Jay, he was fascinated by it. And I think he also fed into my passion for the business. I have to admit—the wrecking business is infectious, and when you catch it, there is no cure. Jay caught it.

Jay and I kind of fed off each other too. While his energy annoyed me at first, it excited me later. And he said the same about me. I didn't come home at night with my shoulders down like I had just put in another day at the salt mine. My work didn't drain me; it energized me and drove me. Jay wanted to be like that.

Jay would hang out with Tammi at night and then get up at four thirty in the morning to spend the day with me as I did my business. While Jay was conditioned from a little boy to be up at five thirty or six because his dad got him up to work on construction jobs, I was even worse. I'd be out the door by five. But he managed to keep up. I'd tell Jay on a Friday night, "I'm going to Richmond tomorrow, and I want you to come with me. Do you want to go?" Jay seemed excited about it. He'd be there ready to go in the morning and get in the car, and we'd talk the whole way.

I talk about Jay talking my ear off. But by this time, it was probably a two-way street. I always liked to dream up new ideas and think of new ways to do things, and Jay wasn't just an enthusiastic listener. He also asked good questions—questions that sometimes made me think of even better ideas. He was a great sounding board.

Jay wasn't shy about asking those questions either. Jay tells me now that he has a daughter of his own, he doesn't know if he would have been so accommodating in my shoes. But I think part of it was Jay and I just clicked. I also liked that he didn't seem scared of me like some of the other guys Tammi had dated. It's kind of funny because what initially annoyed me about Jay turned out to be what I liked most about him. He was straightforward and honest and didn't hold anything back.

Tammi told me later that Jay kidded her once that if they didn't get married, he was going to marry me. I'm not sure how to feel about that, actually. But luckily Jay and Tammi did get married, so it never came to that. And Jay and I were able to become even closer friends.

Be a Good Teacher

Jay was going to college, but he was getting an even bigger education hanging out with me. It was just like the time I spent with my dad—only I was the teacher this time. A typical day would mean stopping at the Sacramento yard, followed by a stop in Fairfield and then Richmond. And in between, there would be food at a greasy spoon and more conversation.

At first Jay was just the tagalong, gofer kid, as he liked to refer to himself, running from business to business getting one thing or another and helping out when needed.

We'd walk through the yard and I'd tell him what you should and shouldn't do if you were going to make the business work. He soaked it up and was a fast learner. I'd point out pieces of salvage and tell him what it was worth and explain how the more expensive ones were harder to find so you could get more. I'd tell him how much I liked a certain motor because it broke a lot. Jay didn't understand that at first; why would a motor that broke all the time be so great? But I told him, "You're never going to sell it if it doesn't break. What are you going to do with a bunch of motors that never break?" It was a big learning curve.

My own kids didn't have the same interest in the business that Jay did. Jason turned out to be the only one to work at the company for any length of time. He was a lot like his uncle Curtis in that he liked working outside—driving forklifts and building fences and taking inventory of the cars. But he didn't like working in the office or looking at spreadsheets. Jay was like me and enjoyed doing both.

Jason loves to rebuild cars, and he ended up having his own collection of hot rods. The only way he thought you could get a car was to fix a wrecked one. He got that from the business and from me. But he doesn't have the passion for the salvage business itself. There's no use in trying to change that, and I wouldn't want to. You have to do what you are passionate about.

Be Your Customer's Most Valuable Partner

My continued passion for the business helped me find new ways to innovate Copart. One of the biggest innovations was the Percentage Incentive Program, or PIP, which I started as a test with the Fireman's Fund—an insurance company that was a client of Copart.

Prior to the PIP program, cars that were badly damaged were upside-down for insurance companies who had to pay us tow fees, storage fees, and seller fees that far exceeded the price they would get on a vehicle. For example, a burned-out car may only get $25 at auction for its remaining metal. But the fees to pick it up, store it, and auction it amounted to about $200, which meant Copart ended up having to bill the insurance companies $175 instead of sending them a check for the profits.

At the same time, I saw potential in getting more money for newer vehicles that could be repaired. Newer cars that were damaged in accidents would frequently sit at a body shop for weeks collecting dust and grime through the shattered windows. Tow trucks picking up cars from accidents also typically sweep up all the debris from the wreck and toss it in the front seat on the leather or crushed velour interior. *What if we could clean up those cars—take out the debris, vacuum them out, and make them look clean and new again (outside of the damage)? They would be more attractive to buyers and get more bids, driving the price higher,* I thought.

I knew I could get the insurance company more money if I cleaned these cars up, but I also knew I would have to charge the insurance companies for that service. That was a problem because insurance companies didn't want to pay you to clean up a wrecked car. To them it was junk. I had to find another way.

I proposed a deal to the Fireman's Fund. Instead of charging fees, I would keep a percentage of the sale price for each car—20 percent on older, highly damaged cars; 10 percent on newer cars.

That meant that the burned-out car I could only sell for twenty-five dollars would only get me five dollars. But I could more than make up for the losses on the badly damaged cars with the 10 percent I got off of the newer cars that could be more easily repaired—especially if we cleaned them up and drew top dollar.

The Fireman's Fund was thrilled because they no longer had upside-down cars and they were seeing their returns go up because the newer cars were getting more bids. And I was watching Copart's profits go up with the returns.

But maybe most importantly, PIP represented a significant shift in the industry. Now the salvage auction was a partner with the insurance company, with the goal of getting the best possible price for each car, eliminating any arguments over fees.

A short time after I introduced PIP to the Fireman's Fund, a large water main burst in the Bay Area, flooding several dealerships and damaging their brand-new inventory. The new cars at the dealerships had been insured by Farmers Insurance—which also did business with Copart. Because the cars had only water damage, I saw this as the perfect opportunity to offer PIP to Farmers as well. We dried the cars out, cleaned them up, and sold them with salvage titles but looking like they were brand-new again. The program was an instant success, bringing in unprecedented returns on the flooded cars. Soon other insurance companies followed suit. Jerry Waters, who I knew over at Geico, agreed to put his company's cars on the PIP program too. Soon he was also seeing higher returns.

But PIP also came with some growing pains.

AAA insurance also went on the program and gave Copart all their cars in the region. But that meant we had to tow their cars a long way, sometimes from Reno. Because I was no longer charging for towing and instead collecting a percentage of the profits, the long tows were cutting into my bottom line. I knew I had to expand if we were going to keep up.

Inherit Good Talent and Keep It

During this time, I had also started to spend more time at Copart than at my other businesses. Joyce thinks I was getting bored with dismantling after years of working in that industry and said Copart presented new challenges and new opportunities for me. She was right. I also saw the potential of opening more Copart yards across Northern California so I could arrange regional deals with insurance companies like AAA to take all their cars from a larger area. My years as a buyer also gave me a unique insight into how to grow our buyer base, which helped improve returns.

Fresno seemed like a natural progression in the Copart footprint. With yards already in Vallejo, Sacramento, and Hayward, a yard in Fresno would allow us to serve a wider area for insurance companies like AAA and cut down on our towing distance. I asked Jay to come down to Fresno with me to look at a yard that was for sale because the owners wanted to retire. Jay still had no official role in the business but was enjoying hanging out and helping me out whenever he could, so he went to Fresno with me. While there, I put a deal together on the hood of a car. The deal included keeping all of the yard's current employees and training them how to run it like a Copart yard.

When you buy a business, you can inherit some great talent from that business. To let that talent go is bad business. I learned to really respect the people who came with the facilities we purchased, and many of them turned out to be great, long-term employees who really helped us grow and do well.

Don't Be Afraid to Admit Something's Broken

Jay helped me remodel the Fresno office in one weekend—ripping down walls, building a new counter, and putting in new floors. Jay was getting more interested in Copart and started asking me about the financial side of the business. Like me, he also saw the potential for expanding Copart across California.

The summer after his first year in college, Jay stopped just being the gofer and went to work for me at the Copart office. But when the summer was over, Jay didn't want to go back to school. Like me, he had become tired of sitting in a classroom learning about doing things instead of actually doing them.

Jay told me he wanted to quit college and become a businessman. And he wanted me to teach him how. I handed him a broom and told him to start sweeping; that was his first step to being a businessman. There were no free rides in life, and I expected Jay to earn his way up in the company.

Jay grabbed the broom and got to work. And when I told him to learn how to drive a forklift, he did that too. Next I had him tackle organizing the mechanic shop.

It turned out whatever Jay tackled, he changed for the good, so I began to trust Jay to do even more.

Jay had initiative and a sense for how to make things better. While driving forklift, he found a way to move cars more efficiently that streamlined the routes, saving time and fuel. He paid attention to where the company was spending money and how we could cut costs.

All through my business life, when I shook hands with people, I would mentally put them in a category of where they could go in the company. I got to be a pretty good judge of people, and I saw that Jay had an ability to really make the company run better. And I thought, *Well if he can do this outside in the yard, how can he improve the inside—the office?* That's something a lot of guys can't handle. They can do the work in the shop, in the yard—but they can't handle the paperwork that comes with the inside of the business.

So I gave Jay the daunting task of running the titling department and improving the DMV side of the business. Jay jumped in and caught on immediately. He changed the process and the work flow to make it more efficient, so titles could be processed faster, and therefore sales could close more quickly.

Then Jay started to handle the front counter and customer service—a natural job for someone who liked to talk to people. He went from desk to desk, learning everyone's job in the office and finding ways to make things easier and faster.

Efficiency is what excites Jay. Looking at something and finding a better way to do it is his forte. And that's something I not only valued but embraced.

I'm not the kind of guy who says, "Look, kid, I've been doing this for twenty years, and I'm not interested in changing." I never have a problem if someone tells me something is broken. I have always wanted to do things better and improve on the model.

Jay tells me I embrace change almost to a fault, though. He was always afraid he—or someone else, for that matter—may give me a bad idea, and then I'd hand over the power to break something that didn't need to be fixed in the first place.

But I never really worried about that with Jay. Our friendship was slowly turning into a partnership.

With Pete now gone from Copart, I found I could trust Jay with helping me run the business, giving me time to juggle my other ventures and find opportunities to grow.

Think Big. Think *Real* Big.

After Jay and Tammi got married, they kept up what was becoming a family tradition of moving into a trailer and lived at the Sacramento Copart yard so they could be close to the business.

Jay loved what he did, and I like to think he liked working with me. But he was still unsure of his future. The business was booming, but it wasn't booming enough to go beyond what I could handle. Jay worried if there would be enough growth for him to keep working his way up in the company.

The company was still very much a one-man operation. I had people in leadership roles, but I was really the one calling the shots. Jay compares it to someone owning three or four hardware stores. The manager may be there most of the time, but it was me who decided the crescent wrenches should be on aisle fifteen because they sold best there.

If people had a problem, they'd call me directly. Jay didn't see the need to change that, even if Copart went from four yards to five or even six.

Jay remembers thinking Copart was a great business for one guy, but he didn't know if it was a great business for two guys. He was wondering if he could take on more responsibility and make more money for his family. That's just how you look at it when you are an ambitious twenty-year-old starting out in life. That's how I looked at it at his age too, when I decided to branch out on my own finally and leave my dad's business behind.

Jay also worried about how he was going to fit in because he knew I liked coming in every day and doing what I did. If he did more, what the heck was I going to do?

Then something happened that changed everything, squashing any doubts Jay had about if the company had room for him to grow. I heard from Marv Schmidt that his biggest competitor, Insurance Auto Auctions (IAA) had gone public and had raised enough money to expand at a rapid pace. They were trying to gobble up as many auctions as they could and had approached Marv about buying his.

I had never cared about the stock market. The stock page in the newspaper was as foreign to me as the sports page and about as useful. I hadn't a clue about Wall Street. But when I heard that IAA was making big moves that could affect my business, I decided I should start to care.

Marv sent me IAA's prospectus, and I read it. Then I read it again. And again. I didn't understand most of it at the time, but I did understand this: IAA had not been making the money I thought it should be to go public. They were in debt. Going public allowed them to raise a ton of money, and they didn't even have to pay it back.

On the other hand, we were making money, and we weren't in debt. Even though I knew nothing about going public, I figured if they could do it, so could I. We had a better company. About the same time, I had decided to expand yet again—this time into Bakersfield. Part of my motivation was to get there before IAA and establish a foothold.

I started to make a deal with the owner of a tow and salvage facility in Bakersfield, a woman named Donna who was getting remarried and moving away. Donna was a fierce competitor with another tow company in town. I wasn't interested in getting in the tow business—just salvage. I made a deal for the entire business and then sold off the tow side to her competitor, a move that drew her ire. To make matters worse, I had to fire her son from the business because he wasn't doing the work. That angered her daughter, who was running the business, and she also quit.

That's the bad part about buying a family business. I talked to Donna and told her we were still friends, and she needed to let the business go and just be happy with her new husband. She did that, but I think there were still some hard feelings.

Jay and I went to the new Bakersfield yard to convert it over to the Copart way. On the drive home, I shared the IAA prospectus with Jay and told him I was thinking of going public too.

Jay didn't know what a prospectus was either and had never even heard of one. He didn't know small companies could go public. He knew what a public company was, but he thought you had to be a multibillion-dollar Exxon-type corporation to go public. In other words, he was about as clueless as I was. I explained to him what I had figured out reading the prospectus so many times: Going public would allow Copart to not just grow—but grow big.

Today, Jay and I joke that IAA is the best thing that happened to Copart because even though they are our competitor, if it wasn't for them, we might never have had the idea to go public.

The more Jay and I talked about the prospectus on the ride home, the more excited we became.

I turned to Jay and said, "I'm thinking I can do this! Let's go public!"

The Copart dream had just gotten bigger.

CHAPTER 6

Lessons I Learned Going to Wall Street

It was a big game of Monopoly, played straight up as you can be. And I knew we were going to land on Park Place.

—Steve Cohan,
former Copart CFO; board member

Know What You Don't Know

It's easy enough to say you're going to take your company public, even if you don't know the first thing about it. But eventually you have to get a team of folks together to do the job. I know what I don't know. I also think it's a good idea to learn as much as you can.

I called up an attorney friend of mine who had worked with us before named Paul Styer. I first met Paul when he was fresh out of law school and went to work with a law firm that handled some of my affairs. Later, when he went out on his own, I became his client. He'd do most of my real-estate transaction work, and unlike most attorneys, he didn't try to drag things out so he could bill me extra. He would just get it done. He was a straight shooter, and I trusted him. I told him I wanted him to come to work for me and help me take Copart public. I think he thought about it all of two seconds. That's what I like to see. I hate to wait, and I like to see folks who make up their minds. Paul told me later he was not having a lot of fun practicing law on his own and wanted a new adventure. Taking Copart public would definitely be an adventure.

I had Jay with me too, and I knew the three of us would be a good team. But we needed to know what we were doing. None of us had a clue about the stock market, so I did what seemed like the best thing at the time. I went down to the library and tried to find a book to explain it all.

When you don't know what you're looking for, it's not easy to find it. I looked up everything I could think of to try to find a book that told me what I needed to know. Nothing. I did a search for this term *IPO* I'd heard around. I figured that should tell me something. But I didn't find a thing. I ended up going through three branches of the library, and at the end of that, had nothing. Frustrated, I walked over to the business section of the branch I was in and saw a guy in a suit wandering around the section. I didn't know that guy from Adam, but I figured it never hurts to ask.

I said, "I'm looking for a book on IPOs. Can't find a thing. Do you know of any?"

He looked up, and I don't know what he thought, but what he said was, "You mean an initial public offering?"

And that's all I needed.

Find Experts to Help

I went over to look up initial public offerings and found a book right away. One book—a little thing from Ernst and Young—but at least I'd finally found a book. I started to read through it and picked up the general idea. It became clear that the big thing we were missing was an investment banker.

I didn't know much about investment banking. That was all Wall Street stuff, and working in a dismantling business didn't have me rubbing elbows with the business suit crowd. But I started to ask around. An attorney Paul knew suggested a guy named Barry Rosenstein, who was building quite a reputation on Wall Street.

Barry knows a thing or two about big business. In the '80s, Barry was a corporate takeover guy for Asher-Edelman. Oliver Stone hung around with him to do research before he shot the film *Wall Street*. Rosenstein had worked around folks like John Kluge, who was once the richest man in the United States, as well as billionaire real estate entrepreneur Sam Zell and billionaire financier Carl Icahn. He could quickly sum up a deal and the people behind it.

Barry and I crossed paths at the perfect time. He had moved to San Francisco to try a different role in 1991. He wanted to build up businesses instead of taking them over. He and his partners were looking to invest in businesspeople with great vision and a fearless pursuit of that vision. His theory was that there were basic industry companies out there that really didn't have access to growth capital. One of these industries was auto salvage.

Well, one thing led to another, and Barry came out to the Vallejo yard to talk to us. He pulled up in his BMW, his fancy suit, and nice shoes without socks. He was all New York polish and attitude. We tried to make him feel at home in the dirt lot, with wrecked cars and junkyard dogs. We brought him into the metal prefab building we were using for a headquarters and started to talk Wall Street.

Barry tells me that when he first sat down, he was convinced he'd really hit bottom. A few years before, he had been doing big deals in New York. Now he was sitting in a junkyard in the middle of nowhere talking to a guy with an Okie accent, jeans, cowboy boots, and grease under his nails. But we got to talking, and he started to understand there could be gold in these scrap cars.

"Barry, here's the thing. I'm not just buying a can of soup for twenty-nine cents and selling it for forty-nine cents," I explained. "I have ten different services that are growing all the time. Think of us like the local sewer system."

Well, that got his attention.

"We're a utility. Nothing can get rid of us—nothing. Two of the biggest businesses in the world are car manufacturers and insurance companies," I went on. "If insurance companies don't write insurance policies on cars, then they're out of business. If manufacturers don't make cars, then they're out of business. They're always gonna make cars, and they're always gonna insure them. We're the guy in between."

I looked him right in the eye and said, "As long as we've got the land in the right place to put the cars on, we can't fail. We are like the septic tanks of the sewer system. You can't have the system without us."

Barry told me later that after our meeting, he called his wife and told her he had just met the smartest man he'd ever met in business. I don't know about that; I'd probably give my dad that title. But I do know that despite the fact Barry and I were so different and came from such different worlds, we still understood each other completely. Barry was slick, and I was unrefined. Barry was uptown; I was downtown. But he liked the way I approached business, and I liked his tenacity. We were gonna do business. And we were gonna make some money.

Don't Play to the Odds

Once Barry was on board, we still had some hurdles. He made it clear that Copart didn't have to be a multibillion-dollar corporation to get in the game, but it did need to grow before it would be big enough to generate investment interest.

Barry told us he could raise $10 million if we could prove we could grow the company with that money. But it wouldn't be easy.

First of all, Barry was already getting flack about helping me out. He told me all his Wall Street buddies thought he was crazy to give me money. After all, I was just a guy who owned a junkyard and talked like I was from some backwater town. I had no GAP accounting and no financials. But Barry believed in me, he said. He saw something in me that convinced him I was the real deal.

But he still had to let me know what we were up against.

Barry said, "Willis, this is the deal. Ninety-seven percent of people who try to go public don't make it. You need to remember what your odds are."

Well, I never have been the kind of guy who played the odds. I take chances. Besides, the odds had always seemed to end up in my favor in the end. And again, I just never thought I couldn't do it. It didn't even cross my mind that I might be part of that 97 percent.

"Okay," I said. "I don't have a problem with that. Let's do it."

Barry started to set up meetings. He put me in touch with John Goodrich, a Silicon Valley lawyer, and Steve Cohan, a top accountant. We met for the first time in a soul food diner in Vallejo.

I walked in, dropped IAA's prospectus on the table, and told him, "I'm better than they are."

Over pork chops and gravy, I convinced them.

Steve told me later that he admired my principles and the fact that failure wasn't an option for me. But while I was driven, I was also willing to wait to do it the way I wanted, without cutting deals I shouldn't or selling myself or the business short. John and Steve respected that, which I appreciated it.

John and Steve are good guys. They stayed with us over a long haul. I wasn't much like the folks they usually dealt with, but I play the game honestly and ethically. They liked that. And it worked out for all of us.

"It was a big game of Monopoly, played as straight up as you can be," Steve told me later. "And I knew we were going to land on Park Place."

Speak Your Own Language

It's easy sometimes to pretend you're something you are not—especially when so much is at stake. I could have probably bought a fancier suit and learned some big words to impress people while we went out to meet investors. But my mom raised me to be proud of who I was and not to put on airs. Also, I'm just not that good of an actor, and neither do I want to be.

Sometimes people underestimated me because of the way I talked and because I looked more like an Okie farm boy than a polished city slicker. Those people usually lost out. It was a good way to weed out the jerks, though—the Wall Street types who would talk down to me, thinking I was less than them somehow. They didn't know it, but as they were judging me, I was summing them up too—seeing if they were going to play honest or try to take advantage of me.

People call my "unusual" twists on the English language "Willisisms," and I don't mind. I may not say things the same way other people do, but that's what keeps things interesting. One time I was at a meeting with some investment bankers, explaining an unusual situation or "aberration."

"It's an aborigine," I said. When the bankers left the room, I realized my error, turned to Jay, and said, "Is an aborigine one of those guys in Australia?"

Jay nodded.

Oh well. They understood what I meant in the end.

Be Careful Who You Go into Business With

Most investors thought it was all about them liking me. But in my case, I also had to like them. I wasn't doing business with just anyone with a checkbook. I have to trust you—and you have to be someone I feel good about being associated with.

When Barry was first trying to raise us money, I sat across the table from some potential investors I knew weren't the kind of people I wanted to do business with or be associated with.

So I looked across the table, and said, "You know what? I don't want your money."

Then I stood up and walked out the door.

Back at the yard, Barry went ballistic. "What do you mean, you don't want their money?" Barry asked incredulously.

I looked back at Barry and said, "I don't like them."

Barry couldn't believe that this was a conversation he was having. This wasn't how things happened on Wall Street, that was for sure. "You don't like them?"

I tried to explain, "Look, if I'm going to make somebody money, I've got to like them."

I've been in business a long time, and if I don't trust people from a conversation across a dinner table, I'm pretty sure I'm not going to trust them with my reputation or my money. And if I don't trust them with my money, I'm sure not going to go making money for them.

I told Barry, "They're not good partners. I don't want to deal with them."

Seemed pretty straightforward, I thought.

"Are you trying to kill me?" Barry was furious. He stomped around the office and then lay down on the floor.

"Barry? What are you doing?" I asked.

"I'm stretching out my aching back, Willis. You are a pain in my … back."

Trust Your Instincts

As I was trying to find investors I liked and building my team, I was also trying to continue to grow the business. My biggest competitor in the Sacramento area was a man named Bob Spence who owned two facilities—a small yard in Pittsburg, California, and a very large yard in Sacramento. Together they made up a company called Sac Salvage. Bob had all the Allstate business in the area, while I had Farmers, AAA, and some other, smaller insurance companies. Although I had five yards, Bob and I had similar profit margins because I was spending a lot of money growing. We also shared a common foe—IAA.

I decided to call Bob and ask him to join forces. If we merged our companies together and went public, we would have a better shot at fending off IAA from taking more business. Bob was interested, so Ernst and Young did an independent evaluation on both companies and found them to be about equal in value. Our plan was to merge and then approach Jimmy Meeks about selling South Bay Salvage in San Martin to us. Our next move would then be to expand up the coast to Portland.

But while Bob and I seemed to be on the same page, I had a strange feeling. Part of it was that I knew Bob didn't like that I had already started picking a team to go public prior to us merging companies. Bob wanted to be able to pick his own team. But the strange feeling went beyond that. Something was happening underneath the blankets. I didn't see it, but I felt it.

My suspicions grew when I went to the lawyer's office for an important meeting that would finalize the deal. I waited in the lobby for a long time, but there was no sign of Bob.

Bob's wife finally came out of the lawyer's office, looking nervous, and I asked her what was wrong. She didn't say anything. That's when I knew.

"Tell Bob the whole thing's off," I told her. And I left.

I still didn't know exactly what he was doing, but I knew what he was doing wasn't right. I was done dealing with him. The more I thought about it, the more I got the feeling Bob was dealing with IAA on the side, so I called my old friend Jimmy Meeks.

"Jimmy, let me tell you what I'm doing. I'm going to take the company public," I told him, adding that Bob and I had started to make a deal but it had fallen apart. "I'm still going to take the company public, and I just wanted to let you know what happened because I'd like to talk to you about selling your company."

Jimmy was equally as truthful. "Well, Bob was here a week ago, and he said he wanted to buy the company. We pretty much came up with a price."

"Well it sounds like you have a deal," I said.

"No, we don't have a done deal," Jimmy said. That was music to my ears. I asked if I could drive down and talk to him, and Jimmy agreed.

I had helped Jimmy and his family use the U-Pull-It name and model to open one of their own, and it had done well. Jimmy respected me and knew he could trust me, and the feeling was mutual.

"Jimmy, look, I'd really like to buy this salvage auction," I told him "But I don't have the money IAA has. I can't write a check for it. What I can do is give you some money and some stock when we go public."

The yards were still technically Jimmy's dad's, but Jimmy's dad had trusted his son with the decisions. Jimmy looked at me and said, "You know, Willis, I'll do a deal with you."

Despite our long-term relationship, I was surprised. "Why would you do a deal with me and not IAA?" I asked him.

"Because I told you the price and you said okay, knowing all that money is my father's. You didn't try to drop the price and give so much to my dad and then give me money on the side to get me to approve the deal, like Bob did," Jimmy said.

Jimmy is the most honest man who ever walked this earth. He didn't like doing business with someone who would do deals behind his own father's back and try to bribe him to convince his dad to sell. Although Jim had helped his dad with the salvage pool, it was still his father's business. The money from the business should go to his dad. From there, if his dad wanted to give him any of the proceeds, that was between them.

I called Paul, and the deal was drawn up the next day. Jimmy's dad ended up giving Jimmy part of the money for helping build the business, and Jimmy and his wife, Sherri, went to work for me to help grow Copart and take it public.

Bob Spence called Jimmy a few days later and asked him if he was ready to sell yet.

"If you want to buy South Bay, you have to call Willis because he owns it now," Jim told him. That news sparked Bob to call me.

"Hey, Willis, we should probably talk," Bob said.

"What for?" I asked. I have to admit, I was kind of enjoying this.

Bob told me he was now with IAA, and they were interested in buying me out.

"I'll meet with you for old time's sake, Bob, but I don't think I'm interested in selling," I told him.

The next day we met, and I told Bob the only way I would consider selling is if I stayed on as the CEO of IAA.

"I become the boss of all of it or I'm not selling it," I told Bob.

Bob set up a meeting with IAA in San Francisco, where they told me I could be president but not CEO.

"No. If I'm not the CEO/chairman, then I'm not going to merge this company," I said. I didn't want someone above me who could fire me at will over a disagreement. "You guys just got a competitor forever because I'm not going to do it."

That meeting with IAA just added fuel to my dream.

Don't Let Your Temper Get in the Way

Barry had since found some investors I wanted to do business with, including Willie Weinstein, a San Francisco stock trader who used to run Montgomery Securities, and Bernard Osher, a well-known philanthropist and former owner of Butterfield & Butterfield—the fourth-largest auction house in the world, which was later sold to eBay.

Jay, Barry, and I also met with Jim Grosfeld, who had been CEO of Pulte Homes for seventeen years before stepping down to get into private investing. I needed someone with his reputation and experience on Copart's board of directors, and Jim was also interested in investing in the business.

We all met at a restaurant—which had become my favorite place for these things because deals just go better on a full stomach. I told Jim my plans for taking Copart public. Toward the end of the conversation, Jim asked me how much I was planning to pay myself to run the company. I don't remember exactly how much I told him, but I don't think it was unreasonable—around $100,000 and a company car every two years. But Jim questioned the amount. "Don't you think you're paying yourself too much?" he asked.

Jay, still young and hot-headed, lost his temper.

"Who do you think you are! He owns all of it. He doesn't even need your rotten money," Jay said. I ended the meeting and left with Jay before eating my dinner. I decided I didn't need Jim's money after all.

A short time later, Barry gave me a call. I was already expecting another lecture and more groaning about the pain I was causing him.

"You guys are giving me a headache," Barry told me. "This guy has a lot of money he can invest, and you are just messing it up for me. I can't do it! You can't just walk out on people who want to give you money!"

"Look, I've told you before, Barry. I'm not making money for people I don't like. I'll do it without him," I said.

An hour later, Barry called back.

"Willis, Jim Grosfeld loved you guys, and he's in."

Jim wasn't in just a little bit either. He ended up being the biggest investor, putting in $4 million.

When we met with him again, Jim seemed like a different guy.

"Why are you so nice and last time you weren't?" I asked him.

"Well before I was trying to get into business. Now I own part of the business so we are friends. I'm on your side now, Willis."

From that moment, we developed a friendship that included Jim being a key member of Copart's board. I also learned that sometimes it pays to give people a second chance and very few things are worth leaving the dinner table in a huff over.

Always Have a Plan B

At first, the investors wanted to have a controlling interest in Copart (51 percent) in exchange for their $10 million loan. But I was able to negotiate that down to 26 percent—partly because of the relationship I had started building with Willie and Bernard. I also had to pay them 8 percent interest due each year and had five years to go public and pay the entire sum back. If I didn't, the investors would become my permanent partners.

The $10 million was to prove I could grow the company because Wall Street just doesn't give you money unless you can prove you can make more.

Another condition of the loan was that I would have to sell my U-Pull-It chain, which had three locations. I thought a scrap iron company would be a perfect buyer, for the combined U-Pull-It locations produced about two hundred tons for scrap each day after all the parts had been pulled and sold.

But I was picky about which iron company I would sell to. My former U-Pull-It partner, Joe Fazo, had gone into business with Bob Spence, opening up a self-service yard in Sacramento to compete with my Stockton facility. They had recently sold off those self-service yards to Schnitzer Steel. As a result, I didn't do business with Schnitzer Steel—choosing to sell my scrap iron to LMC (Levan's Metal Company—now known as Sims Recycling) to avoid any ties to Bob. I approached LMC about buying U-Pull-It, and we came to an agreement. I did all the required environmental studies needed for the deal, and when everything was complete, I met with Bob Lewon, president of LMC and nephew of Dick Levin, the company's owner, to finalize the transaction.

We had a price all set on the table, and I had done everything they asked and finished all the environmental studies. Then we got down to the last day of it, and they told me they couldn't make a decision then. They needed more time for upper management to do more research, they said.

I told him, "You don't want me to walk out of this room without a deal." But he insisted he had to wait. So I said, "Fine."

I knew that LMC was playing me so I'd drop my price. They knew I had a deadline and I needed to sell U-Pull-It to take Copart public. What they didn't know is just how much I was willing to do to meet that deadline. After walking out of the LMC offices, I immediately drove to Schnitzer Steel, calling on the way.

"Look, you know I was going to sell U-Pull-It to LMC," I told one of the owners. "Well, they stumbled. They're dragging their feet. Do you want to buy it?"

The owners said they'd meet me that day, but they were going to bring Bob Spence because he knew about the business. I refused. "If you want to buy it, that's fine. But I'm not meeting with Bob Spence."

I met the Schnitzers—without Bob Spence—at a restaurant in Berkeley and laid out all the environmental studies, reports, and paperwork on the table.

"There's the contract," I told them. "LMC stubbed their toe about an hour ago, and if you want it, you can have it. But you have to sign right now or forget it."

The Schnitzers could see I had done all my due diligence and all the prerequisites were essentially done. They agreed to the $15 million deal on one condition—that they could bring their trucks into all of the U-Pull-It locations the very next day and begin collecting the scrap metal cars. I wrote up the additional terms on a napkin.

"You sign that," I said, pointing to the contract and the napkin, "and I'll call my managers right now and tell them that Levan's trucks are out and yours are in."

The next morning I called LMC and told them they needed to get their trucks off my property.

"Are you going to sell to the Schnitzers?" they asked me.

"I already did. They own the company," I announced.

Schnitzer changed the name to Pick N Pull—a self-service chain that would continue to grow to forty-eight US and three Canadian locations.

It took me just a couple of hours to go from not making a deal with LMC to sealing a deal with Schnitzer, proving again I'm not a man who likes to wait around or play games.

I had a bigger agenda. I needed to get Copart public. I couldn't wait. Luckily, I had a plan B.

Be Flexible

With Jim Meeks on my team, $10 million in the bank, and no other companies to worry about, I was looking at where to take Copart next. I wanted to go to Oregon and try to make a deal with Jim Dougherty, who owned an auction there. This would expand our footprint outside of California and up the West Coast.

It wasn't going to be an easy deal to make, though. Jim Dougherty had once owned the salvage pool with Fred Hopp, a friend of mine. When Fred decided to sell his half to Jim, he had asked me to come and do an evaluation of how much he should ask for it. Jim hadn't liked the number I came up with. In a nutshell, let's just say that Jim wasn't a big Willis fan.

When I called Jim Dougherty and heard from his secretary that he was on vacation with Bob Spence, I knew I'd have to change the game plan. I knew Jim was already selling to Bob and IAA.

I decided to go south instead. I knew of an old salvage pool in Colton, California, that had pretty much been destroyed by IAA. I knew the owner, Ron Cherry, and offered to take over the business. I would lease the land with an option to buy—no money down. And I'd give Ron some Copart stock once it went public.

Ron just wanted out. He was losing money and was tired of fighting a losing battle with IAA, so he agreed. Copart was now seven yards strong.

You Can Never Have Too Many Good People

In 1993 Copart also added two critical players to its executive team—Gerry Waters and Russ Lowy.

Gerry, who was an early fan of the PIP program when he had worked at Geico insurance, had become a good friend of mine over the years as we saw each other at the salvage pool. Geico was about to transfer Gerry out of California, and he didn't want to move, so he approached me about a job with Copart.

Gerry came aboard, and he was a great asset because we needed help on the insurance side and he had more than twenty years in the industry. He had all the knowledge we needed to answer the question, "What would an insurance company think about this?" He's also meticulous about following rules and good about implementing systems and coming up with procedures and regulations. Gerry started in sales but served in several capacities at Copart over the years, including operations and special projects, before he retired from the business.

Russ had been working for ADP in marketing and had done very well for the company. But shortly after ADP lost a contract, Russ was terminated, along with a group of employees who had worked on the account. The news crushed him. He was thirty-four, had two kids, and thought he had done everything right, even being honored as part of the company's prestigious President's Club.

Russ called one of his contacts in the industry, who told him about this company called Copart. Russ ended up talking to me over the phone, and I told him Copart was a small company with a big future that could use his talent. The following weekend he was interviewing with Jay. Jay showed Russ a map of the United States. There were seven stick pins on the map showing current Copart locations. Jay told Russ that soon there would be one hundred stick pins on the map; that's how big Copart was going to get after the company went public.

Russ told me later he thought Jay was smoking something funny. He had just come from a $2 billion company and was looking out the window at what looked to be just a junkyard. Jay was twenty-three, aggressive, and a little cocky. Russ wasn't sure if he should believe Jay or not. But something inside of him wanted to see if Jay was right.

Russ became Copart's first official sales guy and eventually worked his way up to be COO. Russ was a great teacher, which made him ideal in building a training program for the operations staff. Russ and

Gerry also worked together to create structure around the operations side of the business, such as devising systems to pay tow companies and receive vehicles.

Never Underestimate the Value of a Handshake

The next step for Copart was in Seattle. Jimmy Meeks and I wanted to secure a yard in the Pacific Northwest and met with an older couple who owned a salvage pool there and wanted to retire.

The old man was a really ornery guy—so ornery that one time when I was meeting with him, we had to go to the courthouse so he could get back his shotgun, which had been confiscated after he shot at a guy who had broken into his yard.

We agreed on a $1.5 million deal for the yard, and I sketched out the terms on a notepad.

"I'll have my lawyer put this in a contract and send it to you tomorrow, and you can sign it," I told them. Just before we left, Jimmy turned to the wife, Mary.

"Mary, we definitely have a deal, right?" he asked her.

She nodded. "We definitely have a deal," she told Jimmy.

They shook hands.

"Your word is gold, Mary," Jimmy told her.

"Yes, it is," she agreed.

I had Paul send the official paperwork the next day. But three days later, we had not heard back.

I called Mary. "What's the deal?" I asked. "Why didn't you sign it?"

Mary was upset. "I have a real problem," she said. "Right after you guys left, about an hour later, IAA called us. They wanted to know what we were selling to you for, and when we told them, they offered us one hundred thousand dollars more."

"Well that's okay, Mary," I told her. "Just scratch out the one and a half million in the contract I sent over and write in one-point-six million instead. I understand that's a lot of money and you need the money. Will that take care of it?"

Mary was relieved. Her conscience was clear, and the deal was done. Now Copart was in Seattle, the first location outside of California. With IAA already in Portland, Seattle was a strategic piece in being able to service cars up the West Coast. If IAA had gotten to Seattle before us, they would have had a monopoly up there, so Seattle was important to us.

But we still needed to have some presence in Portland. I called a large insurance company with a lot of business in Portland and offered them a proposition. They agreed that if I put in a small yard, they'd give me some of their cars.

I then convinced two brothers I knew who owned Ace Auto Wreckers to lease me about five acres to build a salvage pool. I got five thousand cars a year from the insurance company initially.

My next stop was my old buddy Marv Schmidt's salvage pool in LA. Marv wasn't planning on selling at the time, but when I told him what I was doing and how I was going to go up against IAA, Marv agreed to a deal that included half stock and half cash. He also agreed to come on board as an executive at Copart. Marv's history in the business would strengthen the executive team.

Don't Let (Lack of) Money Stop You

After buying out Marv, I was almost out of money. The $10 million Barry had raised had allowed us to almost double the size of the company. But we needed more.

I had my sights set on Texas, where IAA had just bought Underwriters Salvage—a huge presence in the Lone Star State. I knew we weren't going to be able to get a foothold in Texas unless we battled with them right now. We couldn't let them get a head start there.

I met with a man named Ron Yates with a yard in Houston. Ron didn't like IAA, so he agreed to sell to me for $7 million. Problem was, I didn't have the entire $7 million. So I went back to the investors and asked them for more. The investors saw how we had been able to grow quickly and were eager to help again because they understood the potential involved. This time, they got shares of stock and warrants (the rights to buy stock at a certain price until a certain date) for the $7 million they put up. And the Houston deal was done.

It had been almost a year since we had decided to go public. And with eleven facilities in four states, we were ready. The numbers showed a profitable, growing business to investors. But there was a big yard in Dallas I had heard wanted to sell, and I was worried IAA might buy it.

Jay and I took a trip to meet with the owner—Al Hartin. Al was in his late seventies and a stereotypical Texan—right down to the big boots, the big hat, and the big cigar. He even had a big office with big gold wingback chairs.

I told Mr. Hartin my plans to take Copart public and that I wanted to buy his salvage yard.

"How much do you think it's worth?" I asked him.

Mr. Hartin came back with not just a big price but a *huge* one: "Twenty million."

The yard was bigger than Houston but not three times as big. It wasn't worth $20 million. Jay was flabbergasted. "No way!" he told Mr. Hartin. "You're out of your mind!"

But I still wanted to talk about it. Mr. Hartin bought and sold stock himself and understood the market—maybe even better than I did. He knew if he played his cards right, he could get in on the ground level with stock that could potentially double in value. I also had a plan.

I proposed to Mr. Hartin that we could merge our companies before going public—making it even larger and more appealing. If the public offering never happened, we would revert back to owning our own, separate companies. But if it did, I'd pay him with stock. The $20 million was a joke, and I told him that—but I was willing to give him one million shares of stock.

When all was said and done, Mr. Hartin ended up hanging on to his shares for about two years and sold them for forty dollars per share—doubling his original price of $20 million. He was a smart man. He took a gamble, but he had seen my history and knew what I had done in the past. And he hated IAA because they were gobbling up independents like him and messing up the industry. And IAA was cocky—which he didn't care for. He had always been the operator of the biggest salvage yard in America, and IAA had treated him like he was nothing. If you know anything about people in Texas, you just don't do that. He was rooting for us, and once again, I had managed to purchase a yard with no cash out of my pocket.

Don't Let the Naysayers Get You Down

There was one problem, though. To put the Dallas deal together required time—which required us to delay the public offering by about two months. That was dangerous considering the economy was going downhill fast. Also, we had worked hard to generate excitement about the stock, and delaying it might cool that excitement down.

I turned to Barry for advice, who told me he thought it was worth the risk.

"You'll look better to investors with the two biggest auctions in Texas on your books," Barry said.

There was other negativity on Wall Street we had to battle too. Copart was criticized for not having more educated people on its executive board. None of us—myself, Jimmy, or Marv—had gone to college. Because IAA had just gone public, some also didn't see a need for another salvage business on Wall Street.

But despite the naysayers, I never doubted Copart would go public. If IAA could do it, I knew—just knew—we could.

The next step was to hire another banker to help with the public offering. Barry had previously dealt with Oppenheimer, a leading national investment bank, and had asked them to come in and help raise an additional $20 million. That was small potatoes for a company like Oppenheimer, who was used to dealing with $100 million offerings. Oppenheimer didn't want to waste their time on something so small. One of Copart's other private investors—Howard Berkowitz, the founder of HPB Associates, a New York investment firm—ended up having to call in a favor to get Oppenheimer to agree.

Now it was time to start the road show—a string of presentations to potential buyers intended to create interest in buying Copart stock. Barry and his people joined me and Steve Cohen, taking a limo from one banking company to another investment group to yet another team of investors to make their pitch.

I had no idea what a road show was at first. Steve would have five minutes to talk about the financials, and then I had twenty-five minutes to tell my story and why Copart was going to succeed. At the end of thirty minutes, we'd leave and go to the next one, and Barry's people would stay behind and take orders. Every hour on the hour we were meeting with someone else—up to ten in a day. And it wasn't just in New York, it was in Chicago and Denver and California. It was a whirlwind. We were just beat. It was a grueling pace. But we had to do what we needed to do.

Information contained herein is subject to completion or amendment. A registration statement relating to these securities has been filed with the Securities and Exchange Commission. These securities may not be sold nor may offers to buy be accepted prior to the time the registration statement becomes effective. This prospectus shall not constitute an offer to sell or the solicitation of an offer to buy nor shall there be any sale of these securities in any State in which such offer, solicitation or sale would be unlawful prior to registration or qualification under the securities laws of any such State.

SUBJECT TO COMPLETION, DATED MARCH 8, 1994

2,000,000 Shares

COPART, INC.

Common Stock

All of the shares of Common Stock offered hereby are being sold by the Company. Prior to this offering, there has been no public market for the Common Stock of the Company. It is currently estimated that the initial public offering price will be between $10.00 and $12.00 per share. See "Underwriting" for a discussion of factors considered in determining the initial public offering price. Application has been made to have the Common Stock approved for quotation on the NASDAQ National Market System under the symbol "CPRT."

The Underwriters have reserved up to 200,000 shares for sale at the initial public offering price to certain of the Company's directors, officers and employees and other persons with direct business relationships with the Company. See "Underwriting."

See "Risk Factors" for a discussion of certain factors that should be considered by prospective purchasers of the Common Stock.

THESE SECURITIES HAVE NOT BEEN APPROVED OR DISAPPROVED BY THE SECURITIES AND EXCHANGE COMMISSION OR ANY STATE SECURITIES COMMISSION NOR HAS THE SECURITIES AND EXCHANGE COMMISSION OR ANY STATE SECURITIES COMMISSION PASSED UPON THE ACCURACY OR ADEQUACY OF THIS PROSPECTUS. ANY REPRESENTATION TO THE CONTRARY IS A CRIMINAL OFFENSE.

	Price to Public	Underwriting Discount(1)	Proceeds to Company(2)
Per Share	$	$	$
Total (3)	$	$	$

(1) See "Underwriting" for information concerning indemnification of the Underwriters and other information.

(2) Before deducting expenses of the offering payable by the Company estimated at $.

(3) The Underwriters have been granted an option by the Company, exercisable within 30 days of the date hereof, to purchase up to 300,000 additional shares of Common Stock at the Price to Public per share, less the Underwriting Discount, for the purpose of covering over-allotments, if any. If the Underwriters exercise such option in full, the total Price to Public, Underwriting Discount and Proceeds to Company will be $, $ and $, respectively. See "Underwriting."

The shares of Common Stock are offered by the Underwriters when, as and if delivered to and accepted by them, subject to their right to withdraw, cancel or reject orders in whole or in part and subject to certain other conditions. It is expected that delivery of the certificates representing the shares will be made against payment on or about , 1994, at the office of Oppenheimer & Co., Inc., Oppenheimer Tower, World Financial Center, New York, New York 10281.

Oppenheimer & Co., Inc. **Genesis Merchant Group Securities**

The date of this Prospectus is , 1994

Hard Work Does Pay Off

On Friday, March 17, 1994, Copart got ready to trade its stock for the first time on the NASDAQ.

I was sitting on Oppenheimer's trading floor, which was roughly the size of a football field, waiting for the market to open and for the bankers on the other side to make the announcement that Copart was open for purchase. The opening bell rang, and I could hear people clamoring, "Open up, Copart! I've got buys! I've got buys!" But the bankers were silent.

I was exhausted and on a short fuse. Why weren't they opening up the stock?

Barry, sitting with the bankers on the other side of the floor, and seeing my one-finger salute, knew they had to get moving.

"You don't understand this guy," he told the bankers. "We need to open this. "

Just as I got to the door, the stock opened. The bankers had wanted to open it at ten dollars a share, but Barry insisted they open at twelve dollars. By opening it at ten dollars, investors would have made more money as the stock value increased. But opening it at twelve dollars meant I would get more money for my investment. They had also sold more stock than they had originally been allotted—called a greenshoe. A greenshoe allows underwriters to sell up to 15 percent more shares offered in a registered securities offering at the offering price, if demand for the securities exceeds the original amount offered. The greenshoe option is popular because it is a risk-free way to stabilize the price of a newly issued stock post-pricing.

Jay described it as the most amazing feeling in the world when we went public. I had given up 26 percent of the company for the right to borrow $10 million. But as Copart went public, Copart's share price was valued at $12, with 6.5 million shares outstanding. That put the company's value at between $75 and $80 million.

It's a little unbelievable if you think about it. Two years earlier we had been driving forklifts every day, and now Wall Street was telling us we were worth $80 million.

As I heard them open up the stock, I could feel the weight of the world lifting off my back. All the investors I had now owned shares. They were now shareholders, not partners. I had lived up to my end of the bargain. I didn't owe them anything anymore; I didn't have to pay them back.

I also knew Copart was mine again. At the time, I had three million shares, making me the biggest shareholder, with 40 percent ownership of the company. I could do one of two things—use my stock as currency to buy other companies or go back to Wall Street to raise more money. Now that Copart was public, raising more money would be easy.

All of a sudden, we weren't just a mom-and-pop anymore. IAA wasn't the only public company out there, and the insurance companies saw us as being on equal footing. The whole world had changed, at least in how people saw us. Now all we had to do was keep growing, which was the easy part for me.

Jay and I often talk about that day he, Paul, Steve, and I shared in the excitement of going public. It was a very emotional feeling. It was right out of the movie *Wall Street*—just crazy with people yelling and screaming and fighting and swearing. We opened a bottle of champagne, and Jay remembers going into one of the offices on the ninetieth floor of the World Trade Center and looking out the window at the Statue of Liberty.

It had been a long, stressful road to get there, and we both looked stressed too. I had thrown out my back; Jay had gotten a big cold sore. We were a mess.

Jay remembers, "It was a combination of stress and excitement—like being thrown up on stage in front of a camera after you're told you've won the Publisher's Clearing House Sweepstakes. You're stressed out to be in front of everyone and be on the spot, but you're also excited about winning. We were thinking, *Wow, we're public.* But we had no concept of what we had started."

CHAPTER 7

Lessons I Learned from the Competition

> Do you think if I was mafia I would be selling these wrecked cars for a livin'?
>
> —Richard Polidori, owner of NER

Build a Brand

Now a public company, Copart had the resources and reputation needed to expand its footprint so we could not only keep up with IAA but also continue to be able to give big insurance companies a broader geographical range of service.

Prior to going public, I had been approached by Travis Fuller, the owner of two small yards in Longview and Lufkin, Texas, about buying out his business. I had put him off until we went public because we couldn't afford another delay and because the yards weren't big enough to impress the street. But now I had enough time and money to close the deal—expanding Copart's presence in the Lone Star State.

Jay told me we should now turn our attention to the East Coast. Atlanta was an especially strong market, and there was a yard there for sale. We closed the deal quickly. Then AAA Auto asked me to run another training facility for them in Sacramento. Because the first one in Hayward had proven to be such a success, I agreed.

In the meantime, IAA was gobbling up facilities across the country as fast as they could. I knew from my dealings with Bob Spence that their plan was to acquire as many locations as they could and let the yards still run like they had been before they purchased them, even if that meant they ran on separate computer systems and used different business models. IAA figured they'd worry about converting them into one system later, when they had finished growing.

My philosophy was much different. I felt Copart should grow slowly, acquiring strategic locations and then converting each one over to the Copart system and business model immediately. Jay had already become an expert at converting yards—taking the lead in changing things over in all the facilities I had acquired while getting ready to go public.

I just didn't want to grow to grow. I wanted to build a brand. I wanted anything with a Copart logo on it to run the same way—same computer system, same pricing, same way of treating our employees—so people started relating our name to a certain way of doing business. We spent time converting things over and converting employees over and teaching them our way of doing things because in many cases, the old way they were doing things hadn't been working. That's why they had to sell. That's also why I think IAA's approach to keeping newly acquired yards running the same way was wrong. They weren't fixing what was broken in the first place.

Be a Rebel

IAA's rapid purchase of facilities had an effect on where Copart planned its next growth areas. Often they were able to get to a market before us, which meant we had to get creative.

They were especially focused on big cities, so we looked at more rural areas. The good news about that is it is a lot cheaper and easier to run a yard in a rural area. There is also less competition.

Copart's board of directors didn't agree with my approach. They wanted me to grow like IAA was growing—finding locations in big cities like Chicago.

I decided what they didn't know wouldn't hurt them. I told the board I would look in Chicago, but then did what I wanted to do anyway. A Chicago yard may have cost me $7 to 9 million, whereas smaller yards like Longview and Lufkin were between $1.5 and 2 million. I could have more locations this way. I wanted to be able to build a network of locations so I could take on national contracts. I didn't want just to be able to handle some of Allstate's cars; I wanted them all.

Learn When to Keep Your Mouth Shut

I found a yard in Kansas City. But while closing the deal, I found out IAA was right behind me. We had drawn up a deal with the owner and were in Kansas City about to sign the papers when a secretary came in and told the owner he had an emergency phone call. I thought something had happened with his family or at the yard. But then he came back into the office laughing. He said IAA had just called and wanted to come over that same day to talk about buying his company.

The deal went forward, and IAA never met with the owner. But I realized then IAA had resources that somehow kept tipping them off about my next move.

I learned I had to not say anything to anyone about my plans. Even inside the company, I had to be careful. Information just has a way of leaking out, and I didn't want them to know my business. I don't know how they were doing it, but they were really good at it. Wherever I went, they were there a few days later, trying to get in the middle of my deal.

Look Beyond Balance Sheets

My next stops were in Tulsa, Oklahoma; Bridgeton, Missouri; Conway, Arkansas; and Memphis, Tennessee. The owners who sold to me were different than those who sold to IAA. For the most part, Copart was still the underdog to IAA, which had gone public two years prior. IAA would show up wearing suits and riding in limos. I showed up wearing cowboy boots and driving a rental car. Some owners were wooed by the flash of IAA. Some were put off by it. For other owners, it came down to the bottom line—who would pay more?

I had the advantage there. IAA bought companies the Wall Street way—based on pretax or after-tax earnings. I had my own method based on how many cars the auction sold and the value of the land. I knew what didn't show up on the balance sheet of a private, family-owned company—that many of these business owners used a lot of their profits to buy personal cars or pay salaries and benefits to their family members. Many of the businesses were undervalued as a result. I paid a little more for these businesses, but I was also able to see their potential. With my operating systems and business model, I also knew we could increase profits almost instantly.

The other philosophical difference between Copart and IAA was that IAA purchased the cars from the insurance companies while Copart charged fees to store, clean up, and sell the cars. The advantage of this was Copart could limit its liability and get a greater percent of earnings per investment, since they were putting out less cash. The downside was IAA could show more revenue on its books, which people on Wall Street saw as having more potential.

I didn't care though because I knew in the long run, it was about earnings. The bottom line is: what percentage are you making on your business? If we are pulling 30 to 40 percent to their 10 percent, we are a stronger company.

Don't Be Afraid to Swim with the (Big) Fishes

As Copart and IAA went head to head over where they were going to expand next, I found myself crossing paths with an East Coast salvage company called NER. The company was owned by Richard Polidori, a character who seemed to walk straight out of *The Sopranos*. He chewed on cigars, wore tailored Italian suits with yellow shirts and red ties, drove around in a jet black limo, and flew around in a jet black airplane. It was like being in Little Italy.

A favorite rumor (which was never confirmed to be true) was that if someone parked in Richard's parking spot at one of his yards, he'd shoot out their tires. It was a rumor no one seemed to question, though, as Richard looked to fit the part.

I first met Richard and the rest of Little Italy at a convention in south Florida. I was there with my nephew Rick Harris when we saw Richard making a grand entrance in a helicopter. He had twenty-three yards, so he was a high roller in these circles, and he acted that way.

Of course, that didn't intimidate me. The guy still had to put his pants on the same way the rest of us did, so I decided to go over to the NER group and introduce myself. As we tried to break the ice over a beer, Rick made a comment about their nice watches.

"Yeah, we all got Rolexes and we drive Jags, and life's good," one of the NER guys said.

Rick replied "Yeah, I wear a Timex and drive a Fiesta. But life isn't bad."

That got everyone laughing, and everyone became friends.

Be Careful Who Is Listening

Back in California, I told Jay about meeting the Polidoris.

"Well, rumor has it they are connected," Jay told me, referring to the mob.

"Ah, don't worry about it. That's all in the movies," I told him. "It's all a game show with them. They've got New England tied up, and they're doing very good. They are just having fun, but they're really nice guys."

I decided to approach Richard about selling NER. It would be good for Copart, not just giving us locations on the East Coast but also almost doubling our size. I called Richard, and we agreed to meet.

I flew out to NER's headquarters and sat in Richard's office. Richard sat behind a huge desk with an equally huge swordfish mounted on the wall behind him—a big fish for a big fish.

As we talked, I got even more excited about NER. Copart and NER were almost mirror images of each other, just on different sides of the country. NER had a fleet of Fiat forklifts and ran International trucks—just like Copart. We both used IBM inventory tracking systems and ran our businesses in pretty much the same way.

Richard had even thought about taking NER public about the same time IAA did, but he couldn't stomach the investment bankers, he said. They wanted too much money and too much power in the company he built, so he never pursued Wall Street.

But Richard did like me, and he was at the point in his life that he wanted to catch more big fish like the one behind his desk and take time for personal matters. He had just survived a major motorcycle crash and was dealing with subsequent health problems. NER had also reached the point where if it was to continue to grow, it would have to make a major investment in technology. The time just seemed right for Richard to sell.

So we put together a deal—I would pay him $20 million in cash and $20 million in stock for all the locations, without the land. He'd then lease me the land for ten years with an option to buy.

We basically had a handshake deal that we were going to do this, but I really didn't have the money. I had been growing and was out of money. So I had to borrow it, and I hate borrowing money. So I asked Richard if he'd go back to Wall Street with me and do a roadshow to raise more money in a second offering to pay off the debt. At the same time, he could sell some of his stock. He agreed.

Later that day, we were riding in Richard's shiny black Lincoln, looking for a place to eat, when I called Jay on the car phone to tell him the news. What I didn't tell Jay, however, was that I had him on speaker.

"Willis, aren't they like the Mafia? I mean—do we really want to do a deal with these guys?" Jay asked me.

Needless to say, I was taken by surprise at his response—and the fact that Richard heard it. There was a moment of stunned silence as I tried to figure out what to say. It was Richard's thick Italian accent that finally broke the quiet.

"Do you think if I was in the mafia I'd be sellin' these wrecked cars for a livin', Jay?" Richard asked.

We all laughed. But we also learned a lesson that day—watch what you say over the phone!

Don't Expect the Deal to Come to You

Now that everyone was on the same page—and Jay was certain Richard wouldn't put a horse head in his bed while he was sleeping—Paul Styer flew in to draw up the paperwork. Paul and I were putting together the final details of the deal in a conference room at NER when Richard called me into his office.

"Listen," Richard told me, and he clicked the speakerphone. It was a representative from IAA calling. They were asking Richard to meet them in New York to talk about selling his company to them.

"You want me to fly to New York to see you?" Richard asked them, his Italian accent dripping.

"Yeah, you really need to fly up here and see us. We want to talk to you," the IAA rep said.

"Well I can't do it this week, maybe next week. You give me a call when you get to New York, and maybe I'll just shoot up there and see you."

Richard hung up the phone and let it fly.

"They want something from me, and they want me to go to them?" he said incredulously. "I think they misunderstand me."

Richard and I laughed and resumed closing our deal. On May 2, 1995, Copart officially purchased NER, acquiring twenty-three locations, what would be the largest acquisition in the company's history.

PROSPECTUS

1,650,000 Shares

Copart, Inc.

Common Stock

All of the shares of Common Stock offered hereby are being sold by the Company. The Company's Common Stock is traded on the Nasdaq National Market under the symbol "CPRT." On May 17, 1995, the last reported sale price of the Common Stock as reported on the Nasdaq National Market was $19.25 per share. See "Price Range of Common Stock" and "Principal Shareholders."

See "Risk Factors" for certain information that should be considered by prospective investors.

THESE SECURITIES HAVE NOT BEEN APPROVED OR DISAPPROVED BY THE SECURITIES AND EXCHANGE COMMISSION OR ANY STATE SECURITIES COMMISSION NOR HAS THE SECURITIES AND EXCHANGE COMMISSION OR ANY STATE SECURITIES COMMISSION PASSED UPON THE ACCURACY OR ADEQUACY OF THIS PROSPECTUS. ANY REPRESENTATION TO THE CONTRARY IS A CRIMINAL OFFENSE.

	Price to Public	Underwriting Discounts and Commissions(1)	Proceeds to Company(2)
Per Share	$19.25	$1.01	$18.24
Total(3)	$31,762,500	$1,666,500	$30,096,000

(1) The Company has agreed to indemnify the Underwriters against certain liabilities, including liabilities under the Securities Act of 1933. See "Underwriting."

(2) Before deducting expenses payable by the Company of $750,000.

(3) The Company has granted to the Underwriters a 30-day option to purchase up to 247,500 additional shares of Common Stock solely to cover over-allotments, if any. If the Underwriters exercise such option in full, the total Price to Public, Underwriting Discounts and Commissions and Proceeds to Company will be $36,526,875, $1,916,475 and $34,610,400, respectively. See "Underwriting."

The shares of Common Stock are being offered by the several Underwriters named herein, subject to prior sale, when, as and if accepted by them and subject to certain conditions. It is expected that the certificates for the shares of Common Stock offered hereby will be available for delivery on or about May 24, 1995 at the offices of Smith Barney Inc., 388 Greenwich Street, New York, New York 10013.

Smith Barney Inc.

Genesis Merchant Group Securities

May 17, 1995

Consistency Is the Key

After everything was signed, I called the brokerage firm of Salomon Smith Barney and told them I had just bought NER and needed to raise more money. That much growth was good news on Wall Street, and the firm agreed to do an offering. Richard and I went on our road show, and on May 25, 1995, Copart sold about $30 million in stock—1,897,500 shares at $19.25 per share—which allowed the company to pay off NER and be debt free again.

Now that Copart's footprint was bigger, its headquarters also got bigger, moving from the Vallejo yard to a separate building in Benicia. The Benicia HQ became a critical hub for the expanded Copart brand. I didn't believe in having all the locations run separately. We needed to be consistent across the board, so everything was run out of corporate so we could be centralized. If the price of gas went up or down, we could change tow rates immediately at all our locations at once. This was especially important when you were dealing with national contracts in which you had to show consistent pricing.

After the NER deal was final, my sister Bonnie sent me a special gift that hearkened back to our childhood days playing board games—a limited-edition Risk set. She told me I had conquered the world when we were kids, and I was still conquering the world. NER had put us over the top.

Look for Leaders Everywhere

Leaders from NER and Copart met for a big function in St. Louis to celebrate and decide how to restructure this new company and take advantage of both NER and Copart's strengths.

NER brought with it many assets, including talent. Richard stayed on as a member of Copart's leadership team for a while to help guide the merger of the two companies, and other NER employees stayed on as well, becoming future leaders at Copart.

Vinnie Mitz was one such employee. Vinnie had been working for Richard since he was fifteen, when he and his brother helped out in Richard's Hartford, Connecticut yard one spring vacation putting up fences, feeding the watch dog, trimming weeds, and scrapping cars. At the end of the week, both boys were asked if they wanted to keep working after school. Vinnie's brother said no, and Vinnie said yes.

After about a year, Vinnie also started working on Richard's boat as a sport fishing mate and ended up living on the boat for a summer. Richard became like a second father to Vinnie.

When Vinnie decided to go to college, Richard told him to come back when he was through and he'd match anyone else's offer if he continued to work for him. Richard only had the one yard at the time, and Vinnie didn't see much opportunity there. He went to Cornell to study, but since his father died, school became less important. On his college breaks he always went back to work at NER, where he worked various jobs, like driving a truck, being a loader-operator, and even being a mechanic. When Richard decided to open up a bunch of new locations, Vinnie arranged interviews for some of his college buddies and became general manager of the Marlboro yard. He eventually ran NER's entire sales team.

When Richard sold to me, he was adamant that members of his executive team, including Vinnie, be taken care of. Vinnie wasn't sure if he wanted to work for Copart and had made enough money over the years working with Richard that he could open up his own salvage pool. But he was intrigued by Copart's growth, and since Richard had also stayed on, Vinnie agreed to give it a try. It turned out to be a good fit as he continued to grow with the company, going from the senior vice president of marketing to Copart's executive vice president and then president.

I remember the first time I met Vinnie. Richard had asked me to go to Florida and meet with Vinnie to work out some of the details before the deal was closed. Paul and I flew to Boca Raton, and Vinnie came to meet us in our suite. Vinnie was wearing shorts, a tank top, and flip-flops. He looked like a young kid on spring break, and I thought to myself, *Why am I negotiating a deal with this punk kid?*

About fifteen minutes into the conversation, I knew the answer. Vinnie was smart. He knew the industry very well, and he was very loyal to Richard. Loyalty was a trait I valued.

Whenever I shake the hand or meet somebody, I really size them up. After that first meeting with Vinnie, I thought, *If he'll stay with the company, he's going to be a big leader here.*

Vinnie told me that his impression of me on that first meeting was that of a simple, easygoing guy with a clear vision and who was quick to react. I was a guy who had a lot to get done in a hurry, and Vinnie knew that. In that, we found a common bond.

Admit Your Mistakes

In 1995, Copart began to buy cars and resell them like IAA did. It was an idea that was discarded in 1997 after the realization that it just didn't work. Everyone makes bad decisions, and I'm not immune.

By buying cars from insurance companies, Copart had created an environment where it no longer had the same interests as its customers. Insurance companies wanted top dollar for their vehicles, but Copart didn't want to pay top dollar because it needed to turn a profit when it sold them. The overall market dropped, and we started to lose money.

It was just a bad idea, so we went back to the original model. But the good thing about Copart is even though sometimes we have bad ideas, we learn from them and correct them.

That's the advice I also passed on to Jay and Vinnie: Any time you make a mistake or bad news comes and you're really upset about it, remember there's a lesson in it. Just chalk it up as a lesson, and don't let it happen again. When you lose a customer because you bid wrong, don't get mad at the customer. Ask yourself, "What did we do wrong to not get that contract?" Just like with buying cars—it didn't work, so we learned that lesson and moved forward.

Keep Your Growth Sustainable

Another problem Copart had to deal with at the same time had to do with its systems—which was much harder to fix.

After we bought NER, we were working on three computer systems—one in California, one in Texas, and then the NER computer system. We had been talking about building our own uniform system but kept putting it on hold while Copart concentrated on growing.

But the developing system problems couldn't be ignored any longer. It had reached a point where yards could not talk to each other electronically because the systems were so different. If a customer in Connecticut had a car that needed to be picked up in Dallas, Copart's Connecticut yard would have to take the assignment under their system and then call that assignment into Dallas, where they would repeat the process in their system.

Jay was especially concerned about the problems it was causing, saying it was costing the company time and money and was bound to only get worse.

There was also another pressing problem with the systems—none of them were Y2K compatible. Copart's original system, programmed back in the 1980s, didn't have an option for a double-zero to represent the year 2000. At the end of 1999, the system would have no place to go.

As Jay said, there was nothing more important to us at this time than building one system. He didn't even care if we grew anymore at that point. From a business perspective, we had to deal with the systems. So we slowed everything down and just concentrated on systems. It was an example of how you have to make short-term sacrifices to do what's right for the long term.

Wall Street didn't like this sudden stop in Copart's growth pattern though, and the stock took a beating. The expectation on Wall Street after Copart purchased NER was the company would continue to grow at that rate—something that wasn't sustainable.

Jim Grosfeld, who was on Copart's board, gave me some sage advice: "Willis, Wall Street doesn't care about ups and downs. They hate that. What they like is consistency. If you just make that earnings line just move up a little bit every quarter, every year, you'll get paid a really good high multiple because then they can figure your company out."

From then on, I concentrated on steady growth, and when I thought about buying another location, I didn't try to buy it just because I wanted to grow the company. I bought it because it was a good fit and was in a strategic area that helped fill in our network.

I learned an important lesson, and that was not to grow too fast. You have to grow slow and steady, or Wall Street will make you pay for it.

They always compare you to what you did last time. If you exceed what you did last time, you're successful; if you come in under what you did last year, they don't like you.

The Nine-Month Rule

Building one uniform system for Copart also proved to be a huge and expensive task. Copart hired three different people and companies to develop a uniform system. All three failed.

We had one guy, a computer geek, who really put us in a bad position with our systems, and he ended up leaving the company. Then we hired another guy who hosed us. Then another independent contractor told us for a million dollars they could do it, but we ended up getting hosed again. I mean, it was ignorance on our part. We didn't know how to build a system and didn't understand the size or scope. What we understood was that if a guy said he could build you a system, he'd build you a system.

I think Jay explained it the best: Copart had come from the days where companies only really needed one IT guy because technology was not that advanced yet. Copart was still thinking on that level in which one guy could build the system and get it done.

It ended up that one guy could get it done; we just needed the right guy.

That right guy was David Bauer, who Jay and I met in December of 1995. After an initial meeting, David dreamed up the framework for Copart's new system in his head while walking on the beach. It took him two hours to map it out on paper.

Every Sunday, Vinnie and one of our key employees, Terry Willett, flew from the East Coast to California and were sequestered in a conference room with me, Jay, Jimmy, and David for one purpose—to make sure the new system did everything it needed to do to manage Copart's business and inventory. Then they'd fly back to the East Coast on Tuesday night to attend to regular business.

We'd sit and compare what each system did, what each system called certain functions, and tried to consolidate everything. We built in functionality—what did we need that we didn't have? Then David would build it, and we'd look at it and see if it worked in the real world. We'd test it and argue about how we could improve it. These were pretty intense meetings.

At one point, I asked David when it would be done. We needed it now, and I wasn't good at waiting. When David told me it would probably take another eight to ten months, I wasn't happy.

"Well, put more programmers on it—then we'll get it done faster," I told him.

"Willis, I'm going to give you a lesson in life right now," David replied. "One woman can have a baby in nine months. But nine women can't have a baby in one month. The time doesn't change. That's the way it is."

CAS (Copart Auction Systems) ended up taking a year to build at a cost of $3 million—huge money at the time.

We finished the system in December 1996, rolled out the system to our very first yard in February of 1997, and completed the company-wide rollout by December 1997.

About twenty college kids were hired to travel the country and show people how to run CAS. Each state CAS was rolled out in also had to have separate programming for DMV laws that applied there.

Jay and David were the main drivers in the rollout. Jay was always more technologically savvy than I was. While I appreciated the new system, he really understood it. It was probably just a matter of the generation we were born into.

CAS was a huge undertaking, but it allowed us to be one company on one system. Jay especially understood how powerful these technological improvements were for us. Now he could see how many cars we picked up that day, how many cars we sold that day. It helped us manage our business better and bring it all together.

CHAPTER 8

Lessons I Learned from the Next Generation

What's this www crap I keep hearing about?

—Jay Adair, asking David Bauer about the World Wide Web

Embrace New Ideas

CAS marked the beginning of a technological revolution for Copart—one that would not just change the company but change the industry.

About the same time CAS was being built, in 1996, Jay was sitting in a hotel room watching the news on CNN. The announcer said if viewers wanted to learn more about the current story, they could visit www.CNN.com.

Jay called up David and asked him, "What's this www crap I keep hearing about?"

David told Jay it was the World Wide Web, and people could use it to access information on other computers. Jay was curious and told David to try to secure www.copart.com for the future and get www.IAA.com just for fun.

It ended up www.IAA.com was already taken by a furniture store. But www.copart.com was available. Copart now had a website, although at the time what that meant was not yet clear. Jay thought we could maybe use the site to access CAS from a local phone. We were still all oblivious to what this fancy new toy was all about.

For a while anyway, www.copart.com remained on the sidelines as Copart concentrated on its systems. It wasn't until after CAS was launched that the website really started to become useful.

At the time, all the vehicles being sold by each yard every week were put on a master sales list and faxed to customers. More than eight thousand sheets of paper were being used every day to circulate these lists. Then someone had the idea: "Why not put these on the Internet so buyers can look at them there?"

The idea not only saved paper but saved time and opened up the door for other uses for the Internet. Now that CAS was built and able to keep track of statistics from all the yards combined, those reports could also be put on the web for insurance companies to monitor their cars. Pictures of Copart's locations, along with addresses and phone numbers, were also added to the Web.

Get In on the Action

During this time, Jay had also noticed that more and more buyers were hiring buyer reps to go to the sale for them to submit their bids and save them time. One of those reps was a guy named Brad, who would come to the yard and bid for twenty different guys. He'd charge them $150 every time he bought them a car. He'd get their lists of what they wanted and how high they were willing to bid, and he'd sit there all day and bid for them. He'd make $2,000 to $3,000 a day doing this, which prompted Jay to think, *This is ridiculous. How can we get in on this action?*

The answer came to him at an estate auction in the beginning of 1998 when he noticed many people were calling into the auction by phone to make their bids. The person on the phone would bid for them as the auction was happening.

That struck a nerve for Jay, who thought we should devise a way to let buyers submit a bid online. They could do it ahead of time—like the day before—and then we'd bid on their behalf during the live auction up to their highest bid. That way they didn't have to come to the auction at all.

The idea was still fresh in Jay's mind when he and David attended a conference in Scottsdale, Arizona. Jay grabbed David and left the conference early, determined to work on the online bidding concept.

They went back to the room and designed the entire buyer site, including how the bidding would eventually work on the web. But first they wanted to show the buyers what it would look like and explain to them how the bidding would work. This was an entirely new concept—something never done before. We didn't know how buyers would react to it.

Jay talked to buyers himself about online bidding, trying to educate them about the new web-based technology. At this time, online bidding had descriptions of cars for sale but no pictures.

All the buyers told Jay it was a dumb idea; no one would bid on a car they didn't look at first, they said.

Jay told them, "I'm not asking you to *not* see the car. I'm asking you to come look at the car the day before the sale, and for thirty-five dollars you can submit a bid on our website and not have to stand in the auction all day or pay a contract buyer one hundred and fifty dollars to stand there for you."

Once buyers understood the concept, it took off, and Copart had more than $1 million in online sales the first quarter.

A Picture Is Worth a ... Million Dollars

Something else amazing with online bidding was happening too. One day, Jay saw a car in San Diego sell to a buyer in Connecticut. We had never imagined cross-state bidding, let alone cross-country bidding.

Jay had David call up the buyer and find out how he was bidding on vehicles he was too far away from to come look at prior to the sale. The buyer told him he knew what he was doing, but it would be helpful if Copart put pictures of the cars online too.

That's all Jay needed to hear. He directed David to purchase fifty-five cameras and take them to a training session in which he showed all the general managers of the Copart yards how to take pictures of a vehicle. The GMs went back to their yards and started doing just that, sending the camera disks to corporate to upload to the site when they were done. The process was all too time consuming and costly, so David's MIS team devised a way for the yards to upload the pictures to the website themselves, without having to send them to corporate. At first, only cars in relatively good condition had pictures put on the website. But in about six months, all vehicles started having pictures.

All of a sudden we were doing $10 million in sales per quarter. Insurance companies wanted to know all about Internet bidding, and Wall Street was excited about us. It was an amazing time.

Not only was Jay seeing an increase in out-of-state buyers now, but he was also starting to see people bidding from out of the country, from places like Mexico, Canada, and Guatemala. Copart was no longer just a salvage company; it was also a technology company.

Fill in the Gaps

Copart was still physically growing too. Now that the systems were in place, I had a goal of adding six to ten yards per year in strategic locations between existing yards to not only grow the network but also to shorten tow times and cycle times, which is the time between getting a car into a yard and having it be sold and picked up.

Every time we added a dot on the map, we saved towing. This was especially important because at the time, about 70 percent of our customers were using the PIP program and we were eating the cost of long tows. Any time we saw our towing costs were too high, we'd try to put a yard between locations to improve our bottom line. If we can tow a car 50 miles instead of 150 miles, that's money in the bank.

The new yards would also free up space in nearby existing facilities, which in turn could take in more cars. For example, when I opened the Springfield, Missouri, facility, we drew cars from St. Louis and Kansas City to fill it up, therefore increasing capacity.

During this time, I also learned to quickly build green fields—yards that weren't preexisting.

If there was a competitor in a spot we needed to be in, we'd buy the company out because it was cheaper and more efficient than starting from scratch because the permits and everything already existed. But in a lot of places, there either wasn't a competitor or the competitor wasn't significant or didn't want to sell, so we learned how to build yards from scratch and do so very quickly.

I relied on Vinnie a lot to help me decide where to grow. Vinnie's office was next to mine at corporate, and he would always tell me how many cars he was expecting his sales team to get and give me estimates for growth. I trusted Vinnie because he was very smart. He knew his sales team. If he told me we were going to gain thirty thousand cars in this area in the next quarter, I'd make adjustments to my growth plan so we could be ready for those cars and have the space ready for them.

On the other hand, if Vinnie thought his team wasn't going to close a deal, I would also adjust by backing off any plans to expand in that area because I wanted to keep the company's growth very controlled.

It was all about making the company stronger, without any debt, and having more cash in the bank. We wanted to take care of our employees, the insurance companies, and our buyers.

Make Doing Business Easy

Between 1995, when David Bauer was hired to build CAS, and 1998, when online bidding started, the company had grown from forty-two yards to sixty. Between 1998 and 2000, sixteen more yards were added, bringing the total to seventy-six.

In 2000, I was scoping out more locations when my travels landed me in Chicago in the dead of winter. It was ten degrees below zero, and I remember my ink pen wouldn't even work. I thought, *This is insane! People shouldn't live like this!* I guess I had turned into a California boy.

Meanwhile, Jay and Jimmy were in Minnesota thinking the same thing.

"Willis, I almost shivered to death," Jimmy told me through an ice-caked beard. "Even my boogers are frozen! There's got to be a better way!"

As the temperatures continued to drop, so did the number of buyers who braved the cold. With fewer buyers, returns also dropped. So I had an idea: Why not bring the buyers inside, into a nice, warm building, and show them the cars on television monitors? People would no longer have to follow around auction trucks in the cold. That's when EVA (electronic viewing auction) was born.

We brought the auctioneers inside and displayed pictures of the cars on one screen and the make, model, and other information about the car on another screen so no one had to go outside anymore. Buyers loved the idea, but to make it work, it required a lot of building. We had to build an auction booth inside the building, get chairs and coat racks, and buy donuts. We had to do more interior things than we ever had before, including wiring these televisions up on stands. It took a big capital investment to get people inside, but they loved it. While about 40 percent of people were bidding online, there were still a lot of people coming to the sale at this time.

Never Stop Improving on an Idea

Internet buyers still wanted more. They wanted a way to increase their bids on the day of the sale too. Jay figured if there was a way people could bid online during the sale, we would get even higher returns.

But that was easier said than done. In fact, it was so complicated that David had to spend three weeks at IBM and contract with them to help him design an online auction platform that worked in real time. That was the beginning of VB1 or VEVA—virtual electronic viewing auction.

While IBM delivered and David was able to design a system, it wasn't easy to use. Because VEVA worked with a live auction and wasn't an autonomous entity, employees had to monitor the Internet bidding grid and shout out the bids to the auctioneer during the live sale.

It was overwhelming because so much was going on, and employees had to really concentrate on the grid to make sure they were on top of all the bids. We couldn't have the same people doing it for more than an hour at a time because it took so much concentration. The sales were also slowing down, so instead of doing seventy-five cars per hour we were doing fifty. Some of our sales were stretching to five hours. Our employees were getting tired. David even told me he had people who had to hold hands in a circle and sing Kumbaya to try to calm themselves down. They were begging him to make it stop.

But instead of stopping, it expanded. In the fall of 2001, Jay announced that forty of Copart's yards would have VEVA in the next forty days. By mid-March 2002, every yard that could operate VEVA did, with the exception of really large yards like Dallas, which were just too big for VEVA to work without people's heads exploding. VEVA continued to gallop along—stresses and all—for about a year in almost three-quarters of Copart's yards.

Even in Tragedy, You Have to Move Forward

Around the same time VEVA was expanding, one of the most tragic events in American history happened: 9/11. When the planes hit the twin towers of the World Trade Center and another struck the Pentagon, I heard about it first from Jay, who had been traveling in a different time zone. I wasn't even awake yet when he called and said, "Dad, you need to turn on the TV. America's been attacked."

I got up and started watching the TV, and it just turned my stomach. I couldn't get away from the TV for a while—I was so upset and angry over what I was seeing. We had been in the towers often to meet with bankers and when we went public. We could have easily been there when it happened. I also knew how massive these towers were and what a large scale this devastation was. These towers were like cities with fifty thousand people working there and even more people visiting each day. It was just overwhelming to think of the devastation and lives lost. We had one long-time investor who lost a daughter in one of the towers. It was horrible to think about his loss.

When I was finally able to tear myself away from the TV, I started checking on the company and found out that all my employees around the country who were traveling—either for sales or for regional operations—were grounded. No airplanes were flying, and all the car rentals were taken because so many people were just trying to get home. I had people all over who couldn't get home to their loved ones, including Jay. Our private jet was grounded too, so I did my best to find them alternative transportation and get them home. I learned that from the military. You don't leave anyone behind.

A week later, things were still not settling down. It was already clear that nothing would ever really be the same. But there was a software company we had wanted to look at buying in San Diego. Private planes were still not allowed to fly, so I told Jay, "We need to get along with life. Let's fly down on a commercial flight and check it out."

But Jay and I worked out a deal for the trip. When we got on the airplane, he would sit on one side, and I would sit on the other. If anyone went for the cockpit door, we were going to tackle them. Thing is, when we got on the plane, it was just us and maybe four other American guys who all had planned on doing the same thing if they sensed trouble. If anyone went for that cockpit door, we were all going to tackle them! We all had a good laugh about that. But it just showed how much the world had already changed because of 9/11.

So we flew down to San Diego—not having to tackle anybody along the way—and had our meeting. We headed back to the airport after, and as we got there, it was filling up with these young military guys, all joining the service to fight for our country after what happened. We got to visit with these young guys, and I could really relate to them being as I saw myself in them when I got drafted at eighteen years old to go to Vietnam.

These guys were going to military bases all over, but none of them was going back to Sacramento on our plane. As it turned out, hardly anyone was on our plane heading back, just like it was on the way over. If you took the military guys out of the equation, only a handful of people were flying.

We had also seen on the news that commercial planes all over were being grounded—not because the government was grounding them but because no one wanted to fly. On the other hand, car rental companies were booming. You could hardly find a car that wasn't already rented.

I told Jay people weren't going to fly as much after this. Instead, they were going to drive. If that was the case, they were going to wreck more cars. That meant our business was due to grow again.

I told Jay, "I'm going to call Salomon Smith Barney and see if we can do another offering."

We had been spending a lot of money growing the company, so I thought this might be an opportunity to raise some more money. I talked to one of the guys at Salomon Smith Barney and asked if he thought us doing an offering would be OK even though it had only been three weeks since 9/11. I also told him why I thought this was a good time to grow.

He told me no one was doing offerings at this time. Wall Street had pretty much shut down since 9/11, and although there were people who wanted to invest and there was money out there, everything had pretty much come to a screeching halt. This made me think, *Well, if there's a lot of money out there and we have a good story to tell, this may be the perfect time to do an offering.*

At the time I thought we would probably raise about $75 or 80 million to grow.

It isn't cheap to raise money. It costs about 6 to 6.5 percent of whatever you raise to pay the accountants, lawyers, and bankers. But I had another reason I really needed to do this. I had been out of cash for a while. I was spending more money than we had raised out of the first and second offerings and I didn't want to be in debt, so I had been buying a lot of facilities with Copart stock, treating stock as money.

But buying companies with stock is tricky. If you buy a company that is a corporation and you are a corporation, then everything is OK. But if you buy an individual or an LLC or just the assets of a company, when they take your stock, they have to hold it for a year—which makes it a hard sell.

This is true everywhere but in the state of California. California has a law that they call a fairness hearing. Because of the law, sellers can come to California and go through a fairness hearing, which takes all of thirty-five to forty-five minutes with a judge, who explains the whole deal. If you go through this hearing, when the sale closes, the seller can sell the stock the very next day.

The fairness hearing works for any sale in which the buyer is from California—which we were. I was doing it everywhere. It was a good deal. Except for one thing—California had decided to get rid of the fairness hearing, which meant I wasn't going to be able to do it anymore. If I couldn't buy companies with stock, I definitely needed money.

Don't Be a Cheap Suit

We went out on the road show, which we were used to from our first two offerings. Usually you go from one investment company to another, and you only have thirty minutes at each one because their calendar is full. You have twenty-five minutes to tell them about the company and another five minutes to talk numbers, and maybe, if you are lucky, five minutes of questions. Usually there are also only two bankers in the room to make orders because they are so busy.

That wasn't the case this time. In fact, it was totally the opposite. We'd go into a conference room with fifteen investors, and they wanted us to stay because they had no one else coming in—nothing else to do. We had a full calendar of bankers, though, so we had to leave. The only other person I saw in these forty-story buildings raising money was one gentleman who had a business making leg braces. That was it. When we had finished the road show and were getting ready to price, we had filled our agenda and the greenshoe.

Our next step was to talk price with the bankers, and one of the members of our board, Jim Grosfeld, who had gone through a lot of offerings with Pulte Homes, told Jay and me that he wanted to do the negotiations.

PROSPECTUS

4,000,000 Shares

COPART, INC.

Common Stock
$29.00 per share

We are selling 4,000,000 shares of common stock. We have granted the underwriters an option to purchase up to 600,000 additional common shares to cover over-allotments.

Our common stock is quoted on The Nasdaq National Market under the symbol "CPRT." The last reported sale price of our common stock on The Nasdaq National Market on November 13, 2001 was $29.87 per share.

Investing in our common stock involves risks. See "Risk Factors" beginning on page 5.

Neither the Securities and Exchange Commission nor any state securities commission has approved or disapproved of these securities or determined if this prospectus is truthful or complete. Any representation to the contrary is a criminal offense.

	Per Share	Total
Public offering price	$29.00	$116,000,000
Underwriting discount	$ 1.45	$ 5,800,000
Proceeds to Copart, before expenses	$27.55	$110,200,000

The underwriters expect to deliver the shares to purchasers on or about November 19, 2001.

Salomon Smith Barney

Credit Suisse First Boston

A.G. Edwards & Sons, Inc.

November 14, 2001

"You guys will fold like a cheap suit," he told us. "I'm better at it; let me do it." We agreed, but told him we wanted thirty dollars a share. About three minutes into it, the guy offered us twenty-nine dollars, and Jim immediately said, "Okay!" Afterward we told him, "Jim, you folded like a cheap suit, what's the deal!" But we were laughing about it because instead of raising $75 million, we had raised $116 million—a whole lot more than we originally thought and enough to get us into a big growth phase again.

On top of it, the fairness hearing came back to California, which meant we now had cash and could still buy companies with stock. We were loaded for bear! But we were careful about it. We didn't want to grow too fast. Wall Street likes companies that maintain slow and steady growth—not companies that grow 30 percent one year and 10 percent the next. They like growth to be predictable. We had learned that the hard way, so we were very careful about that. It didn't mean that if the opportunity wasn't right we wouldn't jump; we just made sure it was right to keep the stock healthy.

The thing about 9/11 is that it changed our world forever. It's sometimes hard to move forward after such a devastating event like that. It's easy to be frozen in shock and in fear. But in the end, we all have to move forward for America to move forward. That's what we did.

Sometimes It's All or Nothing

In 2002, thanks to Copart's success in taking auctions online, the company moved its headquarters again—this time to a newly constructed 103,000-square-foot, three-story building in Fairfield, just down the road from our Benicia HQ. Copart had truly grown up.

Then Jay got a call from Russ that panicked him. Russ told him he was at their Shreveport yard on a sale day and only fourteen buyers had shown up. There was a sea of empty chairs and a pile of uneaten donuts. The scene had been enough to make some of our insurance customers nervous that Copart was losing buyers.

But Copart wasn't losing buyers; it had just made it too easy for them not to come to the auction.

Jay had to make a decision. We either had to go back to the way we used to do it or move forward because the in-the-middle option wasn't working. The VEVA yards didn't like the system, and the larger yards couldn't use the system.

Jay started to think about abandoning the live auction model entirely, moving to a pure Internet model instead. Buyers could still come to the yards if they wanted to, but the sale would be exclusively online. They would make their bids through kiosks at the yards instead of in front of an auctioneer.

The system would still be based on a live auction to help preserve the excitement of the sale. Buyers could keep bidding higher if they wanted to, and all the bids would be seen on the computer screen as they happened. Buyers could also make preliminary bids the day before, and the computer would use those to bid on their behalf. The whole process would be faster and simpler, however, because it was online.

Jay told David, "It's virtual bidding, but the second generation." That's how it got its name—VB2.

David built VB2 based on Jay's idea. But I wasn't in on it right away. I had been spending a lot of time traveling, finding the next locations for Copart. While I was aware of the drop in buyers showing up to the yards and realized it was a problem, I didn't know Jay and David had been working on a solution.

"We can do two things," Jay told me. "We can get rid of Internet bidding altogether, so buyers have to show up again. Or we can adopt VB2 and do everything online. Let me show you, and you tell me what you think."

I looked at the VB2 demo and didn't hesitate in my answer. "I love it. Let's test it out in some yards and see how it works."

"Yeah," Jay said, "but if you were still an auto wrecker, would you use it?"

"Jay, when I was an auto wrecker, I was in an airplane going to sealed-bid auctions and live auctions. I spent half my time buying cars," I told him. "If I could stay in my wrecking yard and buy parts on the Internet, I'd make more money than standing in an auction line. Would I use it? Absolutely."

Ask Yourself, "What's My Job?"

David had VB2 built and ready to roll out to the first yards on June 27, 2003. Copart tested the system in Bakersfield first, and Jay, Vinnie, and Gerry Waters personally trained buyers on how to use the kiosks so they could see how the buyers reacted. Because it was easier for buyers to participate and they could do it from anywhere, more buyers bid on each car. The Internet auction also retained the same excitement as live bidding, which kept the competitive atmosphere alive. With more competition, returns went up. In fact, the sale had the highest returns of the entire year. It went over like gangbusters.

We tested VB2 at other yards to make sure it wasn't a fluke and had more amazing results.

Jay met with an auctioneer at one of the yards who had worked for us for ten years to tell him he wouldn't have a job if we kept being so successful with VB2. Even the auctioneer said we'd be crazy not to go with VB2 because he also saw how it worked and that it represented the future.

It was time to make a major business decision. That decision wasn't whether we were going to roll out VB2 to all the yards—that decision was obvious, even to the auctioneers who would lose their jobs. So we had to figure out what our job was. We literally sat in a room and wrote the words, "What is our job?" on a board. We decided our job was to help buyers purchase cars easier so we could get the most money for the sellers. That was our job—to get the insurance company more money. That superseded anything else.

With our job—Copart's vision—clearly defined, we decided to roll out VB2 nationwide.

The Weather Is Always Perfect Online

By the end of 2003, the entire company—now about ninety-four yards—had VB2. It took about ninety days for all the yards to be integrated—an aggressive schedule but one that needed to be followed to mitigate the possible negative effects of such a huge change. For example, we didn't want auctioneers leaving before we were ready to launch VB2, and we also didn't want customers getting upset before they could see what VB2 had to offer.

It ended up very few insurance companies got upset with us for the decision—and no one got upset because of the results it caused. The insurance companies saw the proof in their returns going up. We thought VB2 was best for all our customers.

It was a decision that transformed Copart and the industry, starting with the yards themselves. We no longer needed big parking lots for buyers to come to the auction in person. We didn't need as many staff to deal with the buyers either. And if there was a blizzard on auction day that dropped four feet of snow on the ground, the sale didn't have to be canceled because the weather was always perfect online.

Wall Street and the national press also loved it. In 2003, the Internet was still a big buzzword, and for a company like Copart to use it exclusively to sell cars was not only a novelty but also big news. Amazon.com had just showed the world it could sell a lot of stuff on the Internet. And now we were selling wrecked cars on the Internet—and people were actually buying them.

Our costs went up with the investment we made in technology—way more than the costs we saved in donuts, coffee, and parking lots. But the increased buyer base and ease of use VB2 brought with it sent returns through the roof and made the investment worth it.

Today the decision to change over entirely to VB2 seems like a no-brainer. But people tell me they thought I was pretty crazy back then. Between the newness of the technology, the cost to develop it, and the risk associated with changing the industry that drastically, I should have been more hesitant. But VB2 excited me. I saw its potential. I felt it was worth the risk and the money, considering how big the reward of the increased returns could be. I thought of it as a game changer. And it was.

Defy Geography

People from all over the world were buying Copart cars. Between press coverage and word of mouth, car buyers in other countries started to hear about VB2 and to realize they could bid on cars to use for parts or to fix up and sell without leaving their shops in Lithuania, Russia, or South America. We even listed brokers on our website that buyers could hire to pick up and ship the cars for them. Copart made it so easy that geography ceased to be an issue anymore. And with more buyers around the globe in the mix, returns just kept going up. After VB2 was launched in 2003, 14.5 percent of all bids were awarded to buyers out of the country.

Mexico became our biggest buyer. Some people like to think of Mexico as being behind, but they are not behind at all. They taught themselves how to use VB2 so that instead of driving up to one of our border yards, they could do it from home on the Internet.

Even I was surprised at the extent of VB2's success. I knew it was going to be a success, but I really didn't know it was going to go that far. I was looking at it from an auto wrecker's perspective—that it would be easier for buyers and that it would save them time and the cost of travel. When I was an auto wrecker, if I didn't fly to LA and buy cars, I would lose a lot of good cars. That's how I saw VB2.

I didn't see it from a seller's perspective, though. I didn't expect returns to go up. I wasn't thinking that by making it easier, more buyers would use it—and that buyers from all over the world would be able to use it. With all those buyers competing over the cars, it was a natural result that the returns would go up. That was the kicker for me.

Know When to Shift Gears

Copart began to expand even further, breaking the one hundred mark for locations in 2003 and expanding its footprint into Canada. VB2 became a hot selling point for the sales staff, who showed off international bids to woo new business.

The growth was phenomenal. It was kind of unbelievable because it all seemed to happen so quickly. But it really was a process with a lot of important steps taken along the way.

VB2 also got me thinking about the future of Copart in a new way. Although I always embraced technology, it wasn't part of my generation like it was for guys like Jay. I realized his generation would never want a live auction again. They would buy everything on the Internet. And as the old timers in the car business started to retire, their sons would take over, and they'd want to use technology even more.

I knew that although I had established Copart and built Copart's culture on change and embracing new ideas, Jay and the next generation

would have to keep the company on top of the accelerating t
growth the future was demanding. As a result, I started to
in the company, letting Jay take on the day-to-day vision while I
concentrated on expansion and long-term growth.

Focus on Technology

VB2 put Copart ahead of the technology curve. But it had not just been VB2. The fact that we computerized early, the company developed CAS to share data and keep track of all its inventory, and Jay embraced the Internet when it first came out all led up to Copart being prepared to develop and implement technology ahead of its competition.

It goes to show you that any company today has to pay attention to technology and how the world is changing and incorporate that if it wants to survive. You can't do things the same way and expect to be around in ten years. The world moves too quickly. The moment you snooze, you lose.

For example, AOL used to be the top dog, but now they are on the bottom. No one thought Yahoo would ever slip off its pedestal until Google knocked it off. Then Facebook came in. There's always a young guy out there trying to beat what's already been beat. Our philosophy is always to be on the bleeding edge and to never let those young kids come up behind us and do what they've done to so many industries. We need to hire those kids instead so we can stay ahead of the curve on all the new technology.

In my wildest dreams, when I first computerized my wrecking yards, I never thought we'd be selling a car online every five seconds of every working day. I never thought that if you went to a shipping dock in Lithuania or the United Arab Emirates you'd see hundreds and hundreds of shipping containers holding cars that had "Copart" printed on their windshields because we had buyers in other countries importing them.

But the success of VB2 was not without a cost.

CHAPTER 9

Lessons I Learned from Our Employees

Jay Adair? I don't think I know you. Do you work at Copart?
—Office employee to Jay Adair over the phone

Don't Lose What Makes You Special

It was 2002 when Jay realized something bad had happened to Copart: no one knew anyone anymore. We had gotten so big we didn't have that mom-and-pop feel anymore.

This was especially evident when Jay called up a yard to talk to a general manager one day, and was surprised to find out no one knew who he was.

"Jay Adair? I don't think I know you. Do you work at Copart?" asked the employee who had answered the phone.

Copart had become a much different kind of company than when Jay first started working there in 1989. It was big. It was financially secure. It had revolutionary technology. But the vision and spirit we had built the company on was no longer reaching its employees. The employees, as a result, did not act as a team or feel like they were working together. That in turn negatively impacted the company's progress and its relationship with its customers.

So Jay decided Copart needed a revolution. It needed to get back to its roots.

Look for Ways to Turn Bad into Good

Another catalyst for Jay's decision to have a revolution was when Copart disbanded its fleet of tow trucks and began to contract with drivers instead. This improved efficiency and cut transportation and insurance costs. But the decision—which meant laying off hundreds of drivers—also hurt morale.

Up until 2004, Copart had owned and operated its own tow trucks, including multicar carriers. NER had done the same thing, so as Copart grew, I treated trucks as part of the utilities—what was needed to operate. When I built a yard, I added five trucks or four trucks or six trucks—whatever we needed. Pretty soon we owned something like seven hundred carriers.

A carrier is only good for about three to four years before the mileage adds up and problems start to occur. So Copart had about 150 trucks a year rotating off the fleet that needed to be replaced, which was a major expense. But I just accepted it as the price of doing business.

That was the case until Copart expanded to Michigan—yard sixty-one, to be exact.

I was concerned about putting trucks in Michigan because it was such a pro-union state, and one of the most prevalent unions represented truck drivers. I had bad experiences with unions in the past—and not just at Safeway. When my dad was building houses in California, the union came in and tried to unionize and almost put him out of business.

Then, when I had my specialized Chrysler yard in California, the unions tried to move in again. I fought them on the grounds I paid my employees more than any other facility and treated them well, and my operation was safe, clean, and professional. Most of my employees backed me. They knew they were being treated well and didn't want to have to pay union dues for representation they didn't need.

After I saw my dad go through what he did, I always made sure I knew what the average pay was in the area and paid more and gave more benefits. I didn't want people to leave, and I didn't want them to be in a union.

I ended up squashing the union's efforts in California, but it cost a lot of money. And I knew from other people in the business who had lost their battle with unions that it was extremely hard to run a company with union involvement. I wanted to avoid something like that in Michigan.

I left the final decision to my executive team, however, who decided to continue with the system they knew worked and have truck drivers on the payroll.

Lo and behold, we weren't there very long when we got a letter from the union saying they wanted to unionize the yard. When we got the letter, I don't know how many trucks we were running, but we were probably running high—I'm going to say twelve or fifteen carriers—when we started the negotiations with the unions. Then one evening over the weekend, our facility was broken into, and all of our trucks were destroyed. They cut all the lines, they cut all the wiring, and they just destroyed our trucks because we weren't negotiating fast enough or telling them what they wanted to hear, I guess.

We had no other choice but to use subhaulers. It was the best thing that could have happened in hindsight. We discovered it was way cheaper to subhaul than to run the fleet ourselves. We didn't have to pay for insurance, replace trucks, or deal with workers' compensation. We didn't have to pay for uniforms, mechanics, or maintenance.

About 75 percent of our workers' comp costs were for truck drivers. Seventy-five percent of our liability claims were because trucks were driving over mailboxes or knocking down gates. When we added it all up, it was ridiculous. It's crazy we never thought of it before.

After testing it out further, the company decided to get out of trucks altogether. But they needed to find a way to do it that would be fair to the hundreds of drivers who would no longer be on the payroll. Gerry Waters took the lead in an effort to sell all of Copart's carriers to each driver at a discount. He put together a packet of information for all the drivers that outlined how to start their own businesses, including everything from getting a business license and insurance to lists of lenders that had already been identified as willing to finance their new venture. Copart also promised to favor the new entrepreneurs when choosing subhaulers in the future. Whatever the other local guy towed for, Copart offered to pay more if the driver used to be an employee.

Only about 20 percent of the drivers took the deal, with the 80 percent choosing not to take the risk of running their own businesses.

Copart found that owner-operated tow trucks worked harder. Each tow represented more money for their business, while regular employees got paid the same no matter how many tows they did in a day.

All of a sudden we had people doing more loads in the same amount of time for us—because they were hustling more. They were doing three loads a day instead of two. And they were working earlier and later instead of just punching a clock because it meant more money for them. They were in control of their paycheck.

As Copart progressed, the subhaul program progressed with it. Copart began offering incentives for tow companies, like discounts on cell phones and insurance, to sweeten the pot and attract the best companies.

It again goes back to the lesson that when something bad happens, like the union problem in Michigan, you don't need to panic or get mad; you just need to step back and find a new way. And more times than not, that bad thing that happened will turn into a good thing if you listen to the lessons it is teaching you.

Tell Them You Love Them

There were more lessons. Copart didn't just learn that it could operate better without its own fleet of trucks; it also learned it needed to change the way it interacted with employees.

We learned it wasn't just enough to treat your employees nice, give them good benefits, and hope they got it. That wasn't enough to keep the unions out. We treated the employee nice, gave them as many benefits as we could, and treated them like we didn't want them to leave—because we didn't. But we didn't tell them we loved them; we didn't show them how much they meant to the company. That's where we had fallen short.

This was another reason Jay wanted a cultural revolution at Copart. We had been a nuts-and-bolts company where as long as you got the work done, it didn't matter if you had fun doing your job or liked the people you worked with or even knew why you were doing what you did. That made us into a place that on some levels really wasn't a great place to work because it didn't matter if people would rather work around you than with you. That needed to change.

Jay told managers at a conference in 2002 that from then on Copart was going to be a company that didn't just hire on skill sets or IQ (intelligent quotient); it was going to hire based on attitude—EQ (emotional quotient). We were going to be a company in which people liked their coworkers and had fun at what they did. If that happened, we knew they would probably be more efficient and productive and capable of delivering legendary service. If employees are happy, that translates directly to how we treat our customers and how we can move forward as a company.

Becoming a big, public company, we decided, didn't mean we had to sacrifice having a culture where people worked hard, had fun, and were rewarded for it. Jay remembered how in the early days he was given the freedom to disagree with me and share his ideas, which helped him grow. He wanted all employees at Copart to have that same opportunity. You should be respectful of your boss but not fear your boss or be afraid to disagree with him or her. If you have the ability to speak your mind, the company benefits too because that's when great ideas are born.

We also wanted to communicate to employees that the most important thing at Copart was keeping a clear moral direction. So many people separate different aspects of life by saying "this is life" and "this is business" and give them different sets of rules. But we look at business and life and family as all intermixing. If you are happy at home, you're happier at work and vice versa. If you do well at work, you can provide more for your family.

Jay also wanted everyone at Copart to treat each other like friends and family. If you let a friend borrow tools out of your garage and he or she didn't bring them back, you would call your friend up and say,

"Bring them back or we're not friends anymore." That's the way life is. And when the friend brings the tools back, you're all right again. That's how we want to be at work: Take care of the company, and we'll take care of you. Take care of your customers like you want to be taken care of.

Have a Clear Mission, Vision, and Values

To communicate some of these lost ideals and vision, Copart developed a mission, vision, and values statement to guide its business principles and employees. Its mission was to streamline and simplify the auction process; its vision was to continually offer compelling, innovative, and unique products and services to propel the marketplace forward. And the first letter of each of its values spelled out the Copart name itself—committed, ownership, profitability, adaptable, relationships, and trust.

But it wasn't enough to just hang these on the wall. The mission, vision, and values also became a key element in Copart's training and culture.

The CIC—Copart identity campaign—was also launched and introduced initiatives designed to build morale, teamwork, and customer service standards. The campaign included company-wide initiatives, such as the twenty-four-hour rule in which employees must follow up with customer questions within one day. A weekly cheer was also introduced to bring employees together and build company pride, and employees were also encouraged to wear the company color—blue—one day a week.

At about this same time, Copart also hired two more key members of its executive team. In November 2003, Tom Wylie became SVP of human resources in a newly created position. This addition to the company helped secure Copart's commitment to employees and promised it would never again lose sight of its culture.

In April 2004, Will Franklin was hired as the company's newest CFO, adding stability to that position and a strong resource for keeping the company financially stable and secure.

I also formed the Copart Private Foundation—a scholarship fund created directly from private contributions made by me and other executives. The foundation was set up to help Copart employees' children with the costs of college and books. No one who has applied for the scholarship has been turned down.

My military background and strong love for my country also prompted me to start a program at Copart that paid 50 percent salary to any employee deployed to an active US military campaign. Positions are also held for six months for those who are deployed. This policy earned Copart national recognition from the Employer Support of the Guard and Reserve (ESGR), a Department of Defense organization established in 1972 to promote cooperation and understanding between reserve component members and their civilian employers and to assist in the resolution of conflicts arising from an employee's military commitment.

Get to Know the People Who Work for You

Despite these improvements, Jay was still concerned that the senior management of Copart was still too far removed from the people working in the yards, as was demonstrated when the woman who answered the phone didn't know who he was. As he was talking to a business associate one day, he thought out loud about how great it would be if he could meet every employee personally and travel to all of Copart's yards, which numbered more than 110 at that time.

His associate laughed at him and commented he would never be able to do it. Was he crazy? That was all the challenge Jay needed to prove him wrong. Jay promised all the employees he would come meet them personally at their yard over the next year. The world tour was born.

Jay didn't know what he was getting into, though. The world tour took on a life of its own, and the spirit and excitement that had been lost over the years returned as employees tried to outdo one another by staging stunts, games, and skits for Jay and other executives when they visited. During the 2005 tour, Jay found himself riding a donkey, being arrested, getting dunked in a dunk tank, and dressing up as Elvis. It was an opportunity for employees to turn the tables on executives and put them on the spot—and as a result, the executives became more like ordinary people in their eyes.

More importantly, the world tour also had a powerful message. Jay talked to each yard about where the company had been and where it was going. He told them how Copart's change-centric culture had made Copart a leader in the industry and how the company would keep embracing change and finding better ways to do things.

He explained Copart needed to provide not just good service but legendary service—service that left customers saying, "Wow, how did they do that?" and telling others about the experience. He shared the strength of the company's future with employees and talked about how the salvage industry was recession proof because people would always be wrecking cars.

The world tour really brought the company together. We got to know our employees better, and they got to know us. We got back that mom-and-pop feel we had lost.

But as with many things worthwhile, the world tour was not easy. Jay and Jim and other executives would visit three yards—sometimes in three separate states—each day for a week or more at a time. Sleep was grabbed whenever it was possible—but the show always went on. And Jay exceeded his promise to employees—visiting each yard in just six months.

Build a Company That Cares

Through the world tour, we wanted to create a culture where people were dedicated not just to Copart and their jobs but also to our customers and each other. And we did it just in time.

Just months after the world tour ended, a new challenge loomed for Copart that would test our culture and the company itself. On August 29, 2005, Hurricane Katrina, the costliest and deadliest natural disaster in US history, made landfall.

Copart would have to band together its vast resources it had built over the years—its footprint of now more than 120 locations, its army of more than two thousand dedicated employees, its state-of-the-art online technology, and its redundant and organized network of systems—to respond to the disaster effectively.

If strength is tested by adversity, Copart's strength was tested by Katrina. But Copart passed that test, responding to the tragedy like no other company could and proving itself as a leader in the industry and the clean-up efforts.

I, as well as other executives at Copart, knew about Katrina before it made landfall. We were watching the storm's progression at Copart's control center at headquarters. But like everyone else, we did not know the magnitude of what was happening. When we saw the levies had been breached the next day, I made a decision to run operations out of Fairfield and send Jay to look at the damage close up. I also mobilized our property managers to start looking for space to store the excess damaged vehicles.

It took days to be able to fly into the area. Meanwhile, the manager of the New Orleans yard had made his way to the Copart facility by rowboat and had verified it had not suffered any major damage.

Reports of desperate people with guns arguing over supplies had started to come across the news stations. When Jay finally was able to secure a private plane to go into New Orleans, he made the decision to also bring guns in case they met with any trouble. He second guessed his decision when their plane landed at the airport and he saw army and national guard troops everywhere. He got off the plane first and came clean that they had weapons on board. Luckily, they didn't get into trouble.

They still needed a helicopter to get into the heavily damaged areas, though—and all the helicopters had already been leased by emergency personnel and government agencies. Jay finally found an old Sikorsky from the 1950s. He and other Copart leaders then were able to go to the New Orleans yard and look at the damage themselves. While the yards stood mostly unscathed, they were in awe at the sheer magnitude of the destruction in the city of New Orleans, which was literally a sea of water, mud, and debris. They knew this would be bigger than anything any of them had seen before—or would see again.

From August 2005 to August 2006, Copart processed tens of thousands of hurricane vehicles in addition to the more than one million it did in a normal year. It added two temporary facilities for storage, creating the largest-ever salvage yard out of a 180-acre cow pasture in Gulfport, Mississippi, which at its peak took in as many as eight hundred cars per day. This piece of land that was once home to sixty cows stored almost thirty thousand vehicles.

Copart also expanded its services to include recovery and crushing and mobilized more than four hundred employees from all over the nation to help with the clean-up efforts. Employees and vendors worked in adverse conditions, with Copart providing them with food, shelter, water, and power in a place where such things were difficult to find and sustain. Copart also found a way to extend its technology to hurricane-ravaged areas without power or Internet service via a satellite-enabled trailer hooked up to its database, allowing it to process and sell vehicles while others couldn't.

In the midst of cleaning up Katrina, Copart also had to deal with two lesser but still very destructive storms, Hurricanes Rita and Wilma, which produced tens of thousands of additional salvage vehicles damaged in Florida.

Do the Right Thing

Through the ordeal, Copart did not pass any of its added costs on to its customers. Copart chose to absorb the costs for a couple of reasons—first, because it was the right thing to do. Copart emerged as an important ally in the clean-up and recovery efforts, with many government agencies asking for and receiving Copart's help. One of Copart's first priorities after the storm was picking up vehicles at Kessler Air Force Base in Biloxi, Mississippi, so rescue operations could be made to New Orleans.

Copart also absorbed the costs because it wanted to prove to its customers it was not just a vendor but a business partner they could rely on even at the worst possible time. It went back to legendary service and having a clear moral direction—the elements of Copart's culture it had just reinforced through the world tour.

Everything we did as a company prior to August 2005 was in preparation for Katrina. Without Copart's network of facilities, we would not have had the resources and equipment needed for the job. Without VB2 technology, we wouldn't have been able to sell cars from places buyers could not physically reach. Without uniform systems, employees would not have been able to help out in different yards and know exactly how things worked and what to do.

But most importantly, without the world tour and Copart's recent cultural revolution, the employees would not have been able to respond in the heroic way they did.

Because of the world tour, when we asked our employees to go the extra mile—when we asked them to leave their families and help out in a hurricane yard and live out of a trailer for three weeks at a time and work long hours in the dust and the mud—they did it. The world tour had helped build up that sense that we were a family again and that families help each other in a crisis. Copart's slogan, "A bid above the rest," was solidified by Katrina as Copart proved it was not just a little company anymore; it was a force. It was a force powered not just by money, land, and stock—but by people.

CHAPTER 10

Lessons I Learned Overseas

> I'm going to spend my time with my wife. I'm not going to work my whole life and lose the best thing I have.
>
> —Willis Johnson

The World Is Your Oyster

Thanks to the power of VB2, we had started to see the potential in growing Copart's footprint internationally. If we could sell cars from the United States to dismantlers and auto dealers in Lithuania, why couldn't it work the other way around?

Our first effort in testing international waters was in Canada. Canada was close enough that it was easy to start and build yards there, and there were no language barriers to overcome. Some of the insurance companies that were already customers of Copart also did business in Canada. But Canada also had its own currency and rules for salvage vehicles, making it rich territory for Copart to learn. We opened two yards in Ontario within six months of each other. Later we would add other facilities in Ontario and in Alberta.

In 2000, Jay and I also started to travel to other countries to learn about how their auto salvage business worked. We visited Australia and the UK because they were English-speaking countries. In the UK, we met with the leaders of a company called Universal Salvage—the largest salvage company of its kind there, with about nine locations. We met them and liked them, but it wasn't time for us yet. We didn't feel ready or prepared to go into the UK.

They kept in touch, however. Several years later, when we were ready, we approached Universal Salvage about selling, but the CEO wasn't interested. A couple of years later, I saw Universal Salvage in the news. They had a new CEO—a Scottish woman named Avril Palmer-Baunack, who had been hired to help turn Universal Salvage around after some financial difficulties. I knew from research that Avril's real job was to get Universal Salvage lucrative again and in a place where it could be sold for a profit.

That meant I had an opportunity to reopen the conversation, so I called her to arrange a meeting. When we went to see her in England, we all hit it off immediately. Avril had made positive decisions for the company that were bringing more cars in the door. But Copart had the technology that could take it to the next level. Universal was operating much like the industry in the United States had run more than a decade earlier—with live auctions that limited the number of buyers because of geographic boundaries. It needed VB2.

Make It Happen

As Jay, Avril, and I were negotiating how to merge the best of Universal Salvage and Copart, Copart's board of directors were getting uneasy about the deal.

We had prepared ourselves by going to Canada and had spent a lot of time over the last seven years or so researching the UK business environment and how things ran there. We were ready to go to England. Jay and I knew it was a good move for us. But two directors on the board had a real problem with it. They wanted us to slow down, pay dividends, and just cool it. Well, that's not in my blood or Jay's blood. We told them we were not cooling it and did all our due diligence and decided we were going to make this happen.

While Jay and I were finishing up the deal, we would have phone conferences with the board to try to explain what we were doing and the differences between doing business in the United States and the UK. For example, in the UK, cars that were heavily damaged or burned were considered end-of-life cars and by law could not be auctioned. Instead, these cars had to be crushed and more than 90 percent of them recycled. Universal had big crushing facilities to do this.

Some members of the board were concerned about this and completely oblivious that both Jimmy and I had crushed cars when we first started in the auto-dismantling business. The board members insisted that we hire an expert to advise Copart on how to crush these cars and told us to put the deal on hold until the expert could give a report.

Jimmy went ballistic when he heard this. He said nobody with an MBA was going to tell us how to crush cars when there were two guys who had crushed cars their whole lives running the company.

I wasn't willing to wait either. I called for a vote to decide the deal right then. When pressed, the board didn't want to go against me and be divided, so they changed their mind and approved the acquisition.

Always Have a Backup Plan

While I liked Avril, though, I was unsure if I could still trust her to go through with the deal. As a precaution if the Universal deal went sour, I had also been meeting with Steve Norton, owner of Century Salvage, which had three locations for sale.

I didn't want to buy Century prior to Universal because we could scare off Universal—and that was the big deal we really wanted to make happen. So I had to kind of drag things out with Steve while at the same time not tipping my hand to him about Universal.

Steve saw what I was doing. He was a smart guy, and he guessed I was trying to do both deals without the other knowing. But he was still willing to work with me.

Things got even more interesting when Avril called up Steve and asked if she could pay him to be a consultant on the Universal deal. I didn't trust her to go through with the deal, and she didn't trust me to go through with the deal, which is why she wanted to hire Steve to advise her on how to make it happen. Steve made up some excuse about why he couldn't do it, but it showed me she was serious.

In June 2007, Copart officially bought Universal Salvage. Two months later, we purchased Century Salvage.

Get a Second Opinion

Copart started to introduce its systems, culture, and technology to the UK operations.

Jay brought in a culture trainer to help Copart with the transition and help mediate any differences between the American way and the different cultures of the countries comprising the UK. It was the worst thing we did because they taught us totally wrong.

The culture trainer painted a stereotypical picture about how English people acted and said Copart would have to change its culture to adapt to the people in England.

I was leery of changing a culture we were proud of and had spent so much time creating. Jay was also concerned about how the current culture at the UK facilities was working. No one laughed or seemed to enjoy each other or their jobs. This in turn was being translated to the customers coming in the door. There was no enthusiasm or teamwork.

Finally, I decided to get a second opinion. I called Richard Reese, the CEO of Iron Mountain, who already had operations in the UK. I had met Richard at a CEO group I attended and had asked him for his advice before.

"Richard, what's the most important thing I need to do in England?" I asked.

Richard's advice was quick and direct. "You need to introduce your company's culture there."

Richard went on to explain that in the UK, business was very hierarchical, meaning managers didn't like to talk to people many levels below them.

"That's not the way your company or my company works, Willis," Richard told him. "We need to have that communication between management and the employees—that idea flow—for things to work well."

I heard the same thing from other CEOs who did business in the UK. So we painted the UK facilities in the familiar Copart blue and launched the CIC there. Soon all the UK yards were doing cheers and wearing blue on sale day. Executives also went on a mini-world tour and met with the employees and shook their hands.

We found out that people there loved our culture and really embraced it. When we were trying to be something we were not—to just to fit in—it didn't work. But once we were acting like Copart again, people started to see the benefits.

There's this impression everyone has that people in the UK are stuffy—and maybe some are. However, they are also very top notch, and they really embrace American companies and culture. They are very hardworking people. They just have an environment of high costs, and that's not their fault. But they gave us a different perspective on our business, and we have learned a lot from them. The best thing we did was move to England. It's our stepping stone to the rest of Europe.

Most of the UK employees stayed through the transition, with the exception of some upper management. Avril, who had first said she would stay on to lead Copart's UK operations, also left after she got another opportunity that better fit her skills. Her expertise was to save companies—and Copart didn't need saving.

With local leadership still uncertain in the UK, Copart relied on its leaders in the United States to make sure business overseas was running on all cylinders. Vinnie spent a good deal of time in the UK using his sales skills to develop relationships with insurance companies and make sure operations were progressing and meeting Copart standards. Russ also put in a lot of time in the UK to make sure the yards were set up correctly and running smoothly. VP of Operations and Quality Gayle Mooney, who came to Copart during the NER acquisition, worked on training the UK staff on CAS so everyone was on one operating system. VP of Operations Sean Eldridge spent two years in the UK as a liaison to corporate, moving his entire family there so he could make sure the transition remained on track. Veteran employees took turns spending time in the UK, teaching their counterparts the ins and outs of their jobs. This not only helped share knowledge between continents, but it also developed important relationships between employees in North America and the UK.

It was important for us to establish a strong reputation in the UK that mirrored the brand we had spent so long building in North America. We wanted to raise the standards of the salvage business and really show the industry the value and integrity we brought to the table.

Good Ideas Transcend Borders

Copart also continued to expand quickly in the UK, adding four facilities (two in Scotland, two in Northern England) by acquiring AG Watson in February of 2008 and one additional facility with the purchase of Simpson Brothers in April of 2008.

Then in June of 2008, we hired Nigel Paget to be managing director and take Avril's place. With his senior-level experience in auto clubs, roadside assistance businesses, and insurance companies in the UK, he was a good fit. And his sense of humor and can-do attitude fit into the Copart culture and spirit. He knew how to have fun *and* get things done.

By the time Nigel joined the team, Copart had already set out to transform the UK salvage industry much like I had transformed the North American salvage industry over the past twenty-five years. Only this time, the transformation would happen much more quickly.

In the UK, salvage yards purchased cars directly from the insurance companies and resold them at auction. Copart had already discovered this was not a model we could succeed with when we tried it in the United States.

Every salvage company in England was buying every car; there were no brokered cars. We wanted to broker cars because we knew what the power of VB2 could do for both buyers and sellers, and we wanted to be aligned with our customers' interests. So we had to come up with a plan to switch over to the brokered model and accept the fact that in the short term, people might not like it and we would take a hit financially because we were going to lose some business.

We also knew once we got VB2 up and running in the UK, it would be a powerful tool to convince the insurance companies to try the brokered system.

Buyers already purchasing cars from the extensive inventory in the United States and Canada were given the opportunity to bid on even more cars from the UK on a separate VB2 platform that was geared toward UK currency and connected them with UK transports. Existing Copart buyers loved the additional inventory to choose from, and the power of VB2 created more competition and higher returns for the UK cars.

When insurance companies started to notice the returns the cars were getting on VB2, they were more open to selling them directly at auction instead of having Copart buy them first. They were also impressed by the reach of VB2. Buyers from the United Arab Emirates, Europe, and South America were now bidding on their cars, which was never even thought possible using the old live auction system.

It was still a challenge to get the traditional buyers from the UK facilities to embrace VB2, however. Copart employees had to spend time educating them about how to use it and explain how it would save them time. Once local buyers understood they no longer had to stand outside in the rain at an auction all day and could use VB2 from the comfort of their homes or offices, they were sold.

Learn from Your Past

There were some things that Copart did not change in the UK, however. The UK yards had their own fleet of tow trucks, much like we once did. But in the UK, it worked much better for us. Because of the differences in laws, it was much more efficient to have our own drivers than to subcontract towing there, and we had great drivers to rely on.

Now with Copart UK running smoothly, I had to look for the next big opportunity. I hate being bored, you know.

I noticed that the UK did not have any self-service wrecking yards like U-Pull-It. Yet with the economy there, it seemed like a perfect business opportunity.

I decided to draw on my past and open up a U-Pull-It business in the UK—using land I already had from Copart in York, England. I then opened a second location in Inverkeithing, Scotland. The yards ran just like the ones I had started a long time ago in the United States, only instead of the bright orange logo, I changed it to bright green and added a recycling symbol to help market the environmentally friendly aspect of recycling cars to the public. To cross-promote the business, Copart customers got a 10 percent discount at U-Pull-It for any parts they purchased.

Another change I made to the U-Pull-It UK model was that customers didn't just have the option of picking parts off cars but also to purchase the right to take all parts off one entire car with exception of the battery, catalytic converter, and frame. Customers could schedule a seven-hour period in which they could pull off as many parts as they could. U-Pull-It would stage the car for them to remove parts and would remove the engine and gear box ahead of time due to the weight and size. U-Pull-It would also remove the battery for safety and environmental reasons, although customers could buy it back separately if they wanted to.

For people who were trying to extend the life of their cars in the UK without spending a lot of money, U-Pull-It was like a dream come true. The business took off just as fast as it had in the United States years earlier—becoming an instant success.

Find Your Soul Mate

Even after all these years, I was still at work every day at 5:00 a.m. with the same passion I had when I was thirty years younger. I would come home at night still full of energy, thinking of ways to grow the business. I didn't see a time when that would ever change. Joyce joked I was married to Copart, probably because of my custom-made ring with the Copart logo I wore on my ring finger, replacing my actual wedding ring, which was too small.

"Why don't you wear the ring I got you anymore?" Joyce asked me on more than one occasion. She liked to poke fun of me about it. But she wasn't upset. Copart had been good to both of us over the years. She also knew business was something I thrived on, which is why she always had supported me.

Joyce has been with me through everything. When I would get home from working late, she and I would talk about the business. Sometimes it wasn't what interested her, but she was always a good sounding board for me because, especially early on, I didn't have a business partner.

Instead of watching TV, we would sit up in bed talking until 2:00 a.m. I'd tell her what I was going to do and how I was going to build the company, and she would listen to everything I said and then let me know how she felt.

I learned a long time ago that if you gave Joyce the details—the whole story—she really understood the flow of the business and gave good feedback. I'd always listen to her. She was always a big part of it—as an advisor and a gut check, especially before Jay came along. And even after Jay came along, I still talked to Joyce. She was very supportive of me going to Taiwan for sheet metal, of me opening up U-Pull-It, and of growing and opening other facilities. When she saw how excited I was to take Copart public, she got excited too. If the finances showed it was positive, she was for it. But there were two wrecking yards I looked at she had a bad feeling about. She would tell me that if I was in the middle of a negotiation and we prayed about it and something didn't line up or feel right, I should walk away. And in the case of these two yards, I did walk away. A couple of years later, these yards went belly up. It would have been a bad deal. Her gut was always right. She really helped me make good decisions.

Joyce always told me she liked to hear about my ideas and see me excited about the next big thing I had planned. There was nothing she felt I couldn't do, she told me. That's a pretty amazing thing—when you have someone on your side who feels that way. She knew how much I loved Copart and loved taking it to different places and trying new things. Neither of us really knew if I could ever give that up.

Never Forget Your Priorities

As much as I love Copart, though, my first love has always been Joyce.

While on a trip to the UK in 2008 with Jay and Vinnie, still looking for the next opportunity to grow, I got a call from Joyce. She had gone to the doctor, and they had found a lump in her breast. The biopsy had confirmed it was cancer.

I told Jay right then, "Joyce has breast cancer, and I'm heading home tonight. You've got a year to take the company over. I'm going to spend my time with my wife. I'm not going to work my whole life and lose the best thing I have."

Jay didn't hesitate in his response. "Okay, Dad. Get home and take care of her."

It was another one of my typical quick decisions but one I didn't hesitate to make. I decided right then. My best friend in the whole world had a problem. I wasn't going to let anything get in the way of me being with her. Jay was trained to take over. It was time.

Joyce's diagnosis jarred something in me that couldn't be put back. I realized it was time to put work aside and enjoy the success I made with the people who meant most to me—my family.

Once Joyce got cancer, I knew that even if she beat it, she would always worry about it coming back. And when you have that feeling, you need all the support you can get. Cancer changed both our lives. If she hadn't got cancer, I would still be at Copart; I would have been there until I was eighty. You have to get shocked into it sometimes. Nobody thought I'd retire. I didn't think I'd retire. I thought I'd die behind the helm, at my desk, thinking of where to take Copart next. God had other plans.

Although no one was expecting me to retire, I had been preparing for it over the years because I knew it was the smart thing to do. I had taught Jay everything I could pass on. I had even been taking Jay to a CEO group I belonged to. It was supposed to be just CEOs. When I brought Jay, they asked why there were two of us from Copart. I said, "Well this is my president, and he's going to be CEO one day. I don't want to learn anything he doesn't know. I've got my replacement with me."

As Jay prepared to become CEO over the next year, Joyce and I met with doctors, and Joyce joined a support group for women with breast cancer. Reba and Tammi also rallied around their mother, providing her with support. But it was Joyce's decision alone about what treatment she wanted to pursue, and we all honored that.

Joyce has remained cancer free since undergoing surgery. She's a strong lady. Praying works. We all prayed a lot.

Have a Succession Plan

After Joyce's surgery, I extended the year deadline I originally gave Jay. We had calmed down by this time, and I decided I'd give it more time. We were a public company. We had shareholders. We needed to do this right.

We also needed to start promoting other people and realign the leadership in the company for when I was gone. Vinnie had been promoted to EVP after Jimmy Meeks retired. Jay decided after Vinnie's major contributions to the company—not the least of which was getting the UK division off the ground—that he would be the perfect president to replace him while Jay stepped into the role of CEO. Russ would then become COO, and Rob Vannuccini, who had also come with NER, stepped in as head of sales. Paul, Tom, and Will would remain in their leadership roles to provide stability during the transition.

Also at about the same time, Copart began to expand beyond salvage. The company had a large share of the insurance business, and Jay wanted to find new avenues to grow Copart's already huge inventory of cars. He also wanted to grow the company's buyer base. Even with buyers in more than one hundred countries thanks to VB2, we wanted to reach a larger audience like the do-it-your seller or the at-home mechanic.

Two new divisions of the company were born—Copart Direct and Copart Dealer Services. Copart Direct helped the public sell cars through VB2 without the hassle of selling it themselves. They dropped their cars off at the nearest Copart facility and would get bids from around the world in the next auction.

Copart Dealer Services reached out to dealerships and auctioned their unwanted trade-ins through VB2. All of a sudden, Copart's inventory of nondamaged vehicles began to grow.

Copart also created a broker system in which anyone—even people without a license—could purchase cars online by going through a registered broker or a licensed Copart buyer. The broker would collect a fee for the service. This method was popular with the at-home grease monkeys who liked to fix up motorcycles or hot rods and then resell them. At Copart, there was lots of inventory to choose from that they would normally not have access to.

Registered brokers also caught on in other countries, where some licensed buyers would even open up small locations where the public could come in and browse Copart's inventory using kiosks and then place their orders. These brokers—called market makers—would also arrange transportation.

Copart was beginning to be recognized by people outside of the insurance and dismantling business. The company even sponsored NASCAR and NHRA race cars for a short time to build up name recognition among auto enthusiasts.

When You Leave, Leave

With all these exciting new opportunities developing for Copart, I came to another realization. If I was truly going to step down from Copart, I was going to have to move away. The lure of business was just too great—and it was time for my team to do it without me.

These guys were in their twenties and thirties when I hired them, so they were all young, and they always understood they could come to me for help or advice. I always had an open door. They'd go to Jay too, but they would still come to me a lot. I would never override Jay; I'd just give them any wisdom I had and they could make their own decisions. But I knew if Jay was going to really run the company and I was still in the office, Jay wouldn't be 100 percent in control, and that wasn't fair. Jay was ready to be CEO. He needed to be the last person to talk to. I also knew if I was close, I'd still come into the office. I can't help it. It's a magnetic pull. I'd be having lunch with the guys and stopping in whenever I could.

Jay would also have a hard time taking full control knowing I was right there. But he didn't need my opinion anymore. I knew I had good guys running it. I knew that they'd still ask, "What would Willis do?"

I had fallen in love with Tennessee after building a Copart facility there. I loved the beauty and peacefulness about it—and the friendliness of the people. I started to put together a plan. Joyce and I had been planning a trip with all her brothers and sisters and their spouses. One of the stops was Tennessee. I spent a couple of days in Tennessee, not only enjoying our extended family but also showing Joyce what I loved about the state. Then I started to look on the Internet for ranches there and found one in particular I liked. I was building my case to convince Joyce to leave California.

It ended up being an easy sell. Joyce had liked Tennessee too, and as usual, she supported my decision. My mom, who was ninety-one and who had lived with us in a wing of our house in California for nine years, had originally planned to move with us to Tennessee. But her ninety-plus grandchildren—most of whom were in California—convinced her to stay at the last minute. She now lives in Roseville near my sisters and brother.

Joyce and I moved to Tennessee in 2009, purchasing country singer Alan Jackson's 135-acre ranch. Although I had sworn to never have cows again after a childhood spent milking and caring for them, I now own Black Angus cattle and miniature donkeys.

Joyce and I go outside with our wine and pet the cows and feed them when we feel like it—but only when we feel like it. I'm not responsible for getting up at 5:00 and taking care of them anymore. They are much more enjoyable this way.

Tennessee has truly become home for us now, although we still have our home and vineyard in California and come back for about two months out of the year to visit family. But even my hot rod collection now mostly resides in Tennessee.

We've found a church, made many friends, and are heavily involved in politics. As people in Tennessee hear about what I've accomplished with Copart, I often get requests for business advice. I also have maybe two or three business opportunities a week that come my way, with people wanting me to invest or help them with a business idea. I always get excited to hear about it, thinking about where their dream could go. It's really easy when you have business in your blood and in your brain and you have always been geared toward making money.

But then I get home and think, *I don't want to own another business or be involved in business.* I've done that. The only thing I want to do is be the chairman of the board at Copart and help Jay as much as I can when Copart needs it. I really am retired. I don't want to work anymore, and I don't need or want to make any more money. I just want to enjoy the life I have. It's a good life. Things turned out really good.

I've even taken off my Copart ring—although that was mostly because the humidity in Tennessee makes it uncomfortable.

Have Few Regrets

I have only one regret—that I now spend more time with my grandchildren than I was able to spend with my children while they were growing up. I was too busy growing the business to enjoy them as much as I would have liked.

Copart keeps on growing too and is now also in Brazil, Germany, and Spain. I stayed on as chairman of the Copart board and still have weekly phone calls with Jay. But being in Tennessee has helped me to let most of it go. However, when Joyce and I travel, we still stop at nearby Copart yards to say hi. We also may make an appearance at an occasional Copart conference or leadership meeting, where I still make a point of shaking everyone's hand. It's the least I can do since they are keeping my dream alive.

I don't worry about Copart. I've left it in good hands. Jay and I have a lot of similarities. We are both considered visionaries and dreamers, and Jay proved it when he dreamed up VB2. We are also bottom line oriented and care about the employees. But Jay is the leader Copart needs now. He has a real grasp of technology and where it can take the company, and so does Vinnie.

I couldn't have picked a better person than Jay to take the reins of the company I built. The way it sits now, the company is poised to grow, not stand still. But you have to be careful with how you grow too.

One thing I've taught all the executives in the company is that while you may be good in our business, that doesn't mean you are good in any other business. Don't get a big head and think you know it all, because that's when you'll lose. You're really good in the car business. You're really good in the recycling business. You're not necessarily good in everything else, and you need to understand that. Stay with what you are good at, venture out if you see an opportunity, but pull your horns in if you make a mistake.

I admire Jay because he is not afraid to admit his mistakes and learn from them. If Jay tries something and it doesn't work, he shuts it down. He's very open about his mistakes. I remember him telling me a couple of times, "Boy, that was stupid." But the great thing about being change-centric is you can always change back.

I'm glad Jay still is willing to take chances, though—just like I did. Taking chances and changing things up made Copart what it is today. It's the spirit of the company, and that spirit will never change.

One of the biggest changes Jay instigated after becoming CEO was moving Copart's headquarters to Dallas in 2011 and 2012. It was another example of taking a bad circumstance and changing it for the better. The economy took a real dump, and California was especially hit hard. We have a government that doesn't understand how business works, and we don't know from one year to the next what our tax liability is. Copart wasn't alone in thinking about pulling back on expansion, slowing growth, and hunkering down to make sure the company was running as efficiently as possible.

Part of that efficiency was to centralize Copart's headquarters in the middle of the country, where it could respond to customers faster. The move also allowed Copart to get rid of its corporate jets since travel time was reduced because they no longer had to fly across America as often. It was also closer to fly to Europe. The economy in Texas was also more business friendly.

California will always be our home on many levels. We started there, we grew up there, and we still have fantastic facilities there.

But it just made more sense for us to be in Texas as we continued to grow.

Jay's decision was also fueled by the fact that a medical company approached him unsolicited about buying Copart's company's headquarters in Fairfield. It was a sign. I told Jay it seemed like God was trying to tell him something: that this was the right decision.

Give Your Life to God

My faith in God is one of the reasons for my success. I have always put my life and my businesses in God's hands, and God has blessed me and my family. As a result, I have always tithed to various church organizations and am a strong supporter of the Promise Keepers, a Christian evangelical ministry dedicated to uniting men to become godly influences in the world. I give primarily to organizations that have roots in God because I believe people who win on earth can still lose their souls—which means they've lost everything. I want to give others the opportunity to know the joys and rewards of giving their lives to God.

The legacy I think I leave is that I've always dedicated everything I've done in business to the leadership of the Lord, trusting him to guide our company in the right direction and help me make the right decisions. Most of the people in the company know we put the Lord first and the company second—and He's always blessed us, even in hard times. The Lord brings the right people to you, and they touch you. And you have the power to touch people too. You never know when you will touch the right person.

I went to high school. I didn't go to college. How do you take a guy who went to high school, give him a junkyard, and he turns it into a multibillion-dollar company? That's unheard of. And to say I did it all on my own—well, I just don't think I'm that smart. Things just happened, and the Lord gave me common sense to see the future in our business and foresight into the best place to put our investments. My nickname is Lucky Dog, but it isn't just luck. There's something guiding you. And to me, I think the Lord has always blessed this company and the family.

ABOUT THE AUTHOR

I'm a former journalist and newspaper editor who joined Copart in 2005 as the company's first communications manager. I worked at Copart for five years with Willis, Jay, and Vinnie and am proud to be part of some of the events mentioned in this book, including the world tour, the launch of Copart Direct and Copart Dealer Services, and the launch of Copart in the UK. I also wrote an award-winning annual report in 2006 dedicated to Copart employees for their valiant efforts in cleaning up tens of thousands of cars in the wake of Hurricane Katrina. It was one of countless of examples of how the employees at Copart go above and beyond for the company they love.

I left Copart when the company moved its headquarters to Dallas, but Copart will always be in my blood. Just like Willis feels God had a hand in Copart's success, I also feel some higher power guided me to Copart. For that I am eternally grateful.

When Willis called me and asked me to write his story, it was the biggest honor of my life. But I was also terrified. I had never written a book before. Willis told me, "Well, I never took a company public before either when I took Copart public, and that turned out okay. I figure we'll just learn how to do it together."

Willis believed in me, just like he's believed in people before me who were able to achieve more than they thought they could because of him. My single greatest worry during this whole project was that I would let him down somehow. I hope I was able to capture his vision in this book. And although I also hoped to do his legacy justice, I realize now that is probably impossible. Willis's humility makes it hard to show just how brilliant and amazing his accomplishments are—and just how many people he's positively influenced along the way.

I'd like to thank Willis for trusting me with his story and opening up about areas of his life I had not known before. I learned some amazing lessons from him—and I hope those that read this book will also walk away with some of his wisdom and apply it in their own lives.

I'd also like to thank my husband and best friend, Jeff Protteau, whose love and support as I worked on the book on weekends and nights around my "regular job" kept me motivated and focused. Willis often mentions how a supportive spouse is one of the keys to success, and I couldn't agree more.

—Marla J. Pugh

CPSIA information can be obtained at www.ICGtesting.com
Printed in the USA
BVOW02*2235251214

380873BV00002BA/15/P

9 781490 816593